Ng Teng Fong Roof Garden Commission:
Shilpa Gupta
Edited by Adele Tan

The latest title in this book series presents Indian artist Shilpa Gupta's monumental inflatable sculpture, *Untitled* (2023). The sculpture depicts the dualities of our innermost struggles and the externalities around us. This book includes a curatorial essay that situates Gupta's new work in relation to her art practice and other global sociopolitical forces as well as a full colour photo documentation of the sculpture against the backdrop of Singapore's skyline. It also features a guest essay written by a well-known mental health professional who engages with the artist's take on the human condition.

Accompanying the catalogue is a book titled *Artivities: Exploring Inner & Outer Worlds through Art*, filled with illustrated "artivity" sheets. These sheets, collaboratively developed by the artist and a therapist, assist both children and adults in navigating their emotions and responses towards conflict and other challenging issues.

Untitled (2023)

SHILPA GUPTA

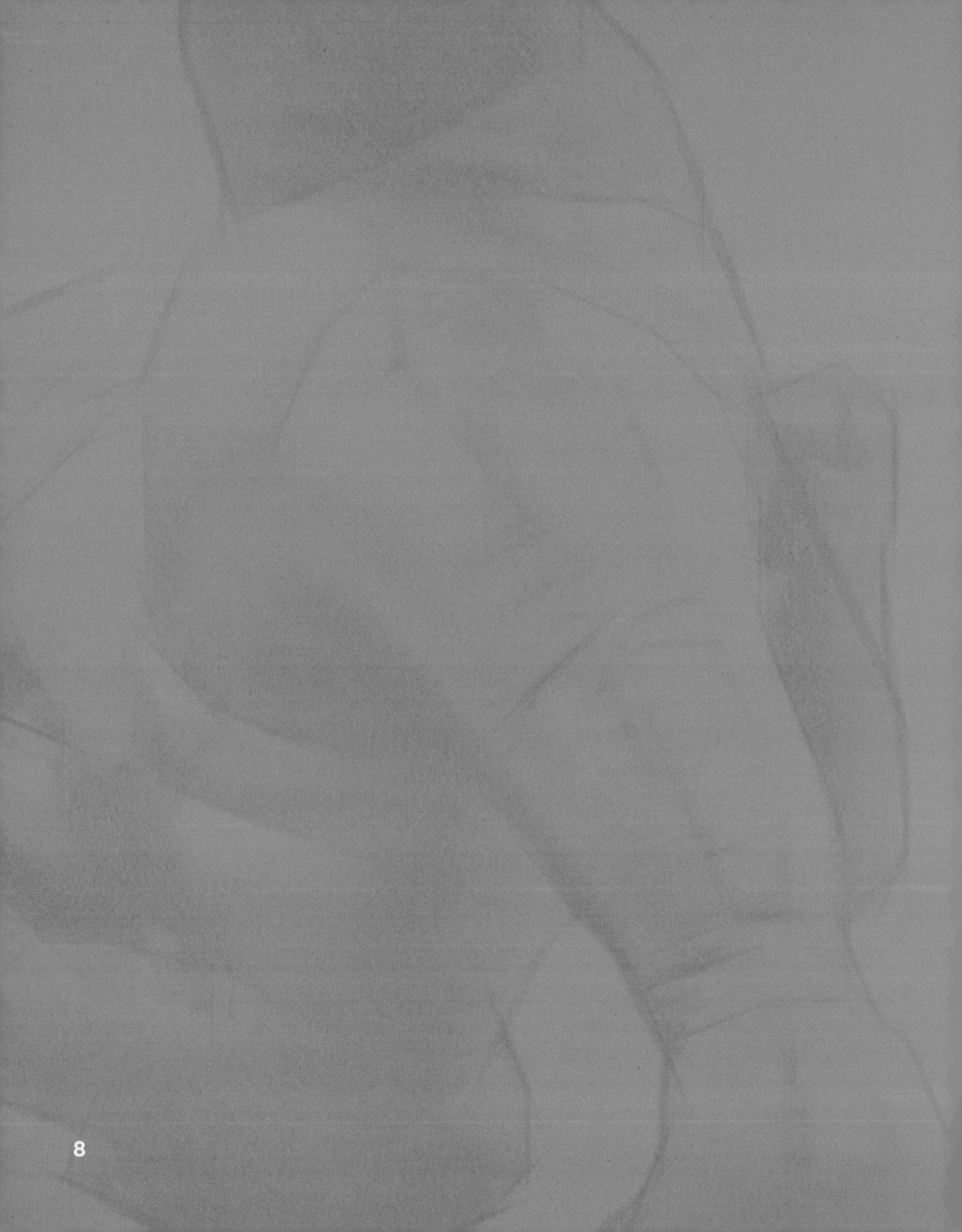

FOREWORD

EUGENE TAN, DIRECTOR
NATIONAL GALLERY SINGAPORE

Shilpa Gupta's *Untitled* (2023) is the sixth installation to feature in the Ng Teng Fong Roof Garden Commission, a series which invites a leading artist to create a new site-specific work in response to the Gallery's architecture and location within Singapore and Southeast Asia. The fluidity of these geographical, social and political boundaries is consonant with Gupta's practice, which has long explored the ambiguity of such forces that define our lives. Personal and geopolitical partitions have had a significant influence on her work: Gupta was born in Mumbai, India, and raised in a conservative society governed by tradition. As a result, Gupta has honed a heightened awareness to the lines drawn for herself and others, the intangibility of their edges and the problematics of such predetermined pathways.

Untitled (2023) explores a different dimension of Gupta's practice. It is a solidly black inflatable that gives little of itself away from afar, but reveals upon closer scrutiny that there are two grappling, interlocked bodies with legs flung energetically into the air and surprisingly resting only on a single head. The figures embody the antagonisms within geopolitical conflict that she has consistently pointed to, and in personifying these tensions, the artist has welcomed a host of other interpretations for her sculpture. In this publication, senior curator Adele Tan anatomises the sculpture to correlate each of its parts to fitting social, aesthetic and psychological contexts. Her interpretive readings trace the origins of the attributes of *Untitled* (2023) through Gupta's artistic practice and reveal the sculpture's possible formal and thematic relationships with Burmese chimera, player mechanics in video games and sculpture in Singapore. However commanding its physicality, Tan ultimately returns to the sculpture's psychological undertows, reading in its bodily articulation the manifestation of interiority.

But whose interiority? Gupta and Tan recognise that multifarious interpretations of the sculpture possibly speak louder of the viewer than of the object. The artist and curator invited noted psychiatrist Professor Dr. Chong Siow Ann to provide a specialist perspective on the intersections between art and psychology, but his fascinating contribution goes even further to explicate the history of mind-body dualism and its implications on his profession today. Dr. Chong's essay records his conversation with the artist, illuminating the artist's own motivations, and underscoring the work's subjectivity.

Nowhere is Gupta's embrace of the ambiguities of *Untitled* (2023) more apparent than in the inclusion of child-friendly activities around the sculpture. Subverting the conventions of monumental sculpture, Gupta devised the sculpture as an inflatable so that it can be touched, especially encouraging interaction from the youngest of our audiences. The sculpture's inherent tensions are infused with a sense of literal and metaphorical levity to provide a gentle starting point for anyone approaching the difficult questions that the sculpture asks of us.

National Gallery Singapore is deeply encouraged by and grateful for Shilpa Gupta's *Untitled* (2023) in Singapore. Heartfelt thanks goes to the artist, her studio and my colleagues at the Gallery for their commitment to this project. Our sincerest gratitude also goes to Series Partner Far East Organization for their continued support of the Ng Teng Fong Roof Garden Commission, which has allowed us to bring such thought-provoking works of art as Gupta's to audiences in Singapore.

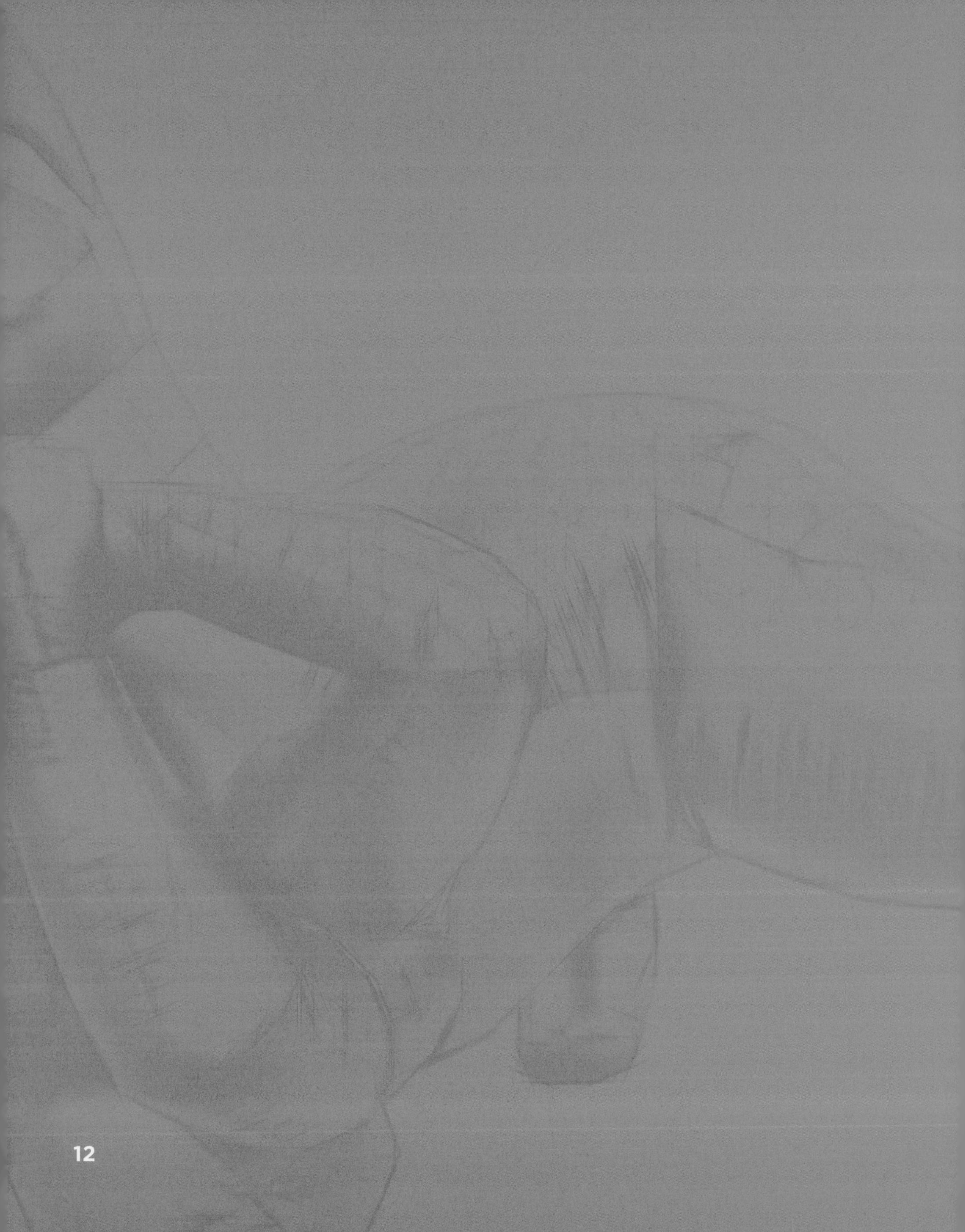

SUBJECTS AT ODDS:

Shilpa Gupta's *Untitled* (2023) in four parts

ADELE TAN, SENIOR CURATOR
NATIONAL GALLERY SINGAPORE

ONE. (Legs)

Two basalt-black inverted bodies are interlocked with legs in the air and attempting to regain balance. Their bent torsos meet in the middle, surreptitiously melding into a single head, like the rarest of conjoined twins. This is the Indian artist Shilpa Gupta's *Untitled* (2023), a sculpture of monumental proportions commissioned for the Ng Teng Fong Roof Garden at National Gallery Singapore. Its scale was made possible by a subversive approach—replacing traditional mediums like clay, metal or stone with malleable vinyl-coated polyester. The result is an inflatable sculpture, preposterously large, yet indelibly soft and inviting. The artist wants to upend the heroic and the historical, the semantic and categorical burdens that most figurative forms bear. On the horizon of the Garden's deck, sculpture is literally turned on its head.

But the genealogy of plastic forms is not the artist's main target of reckoning. Instead, her project had more prosaic beginnings, drawing inspiration from a found photograph of two wrestlers locked

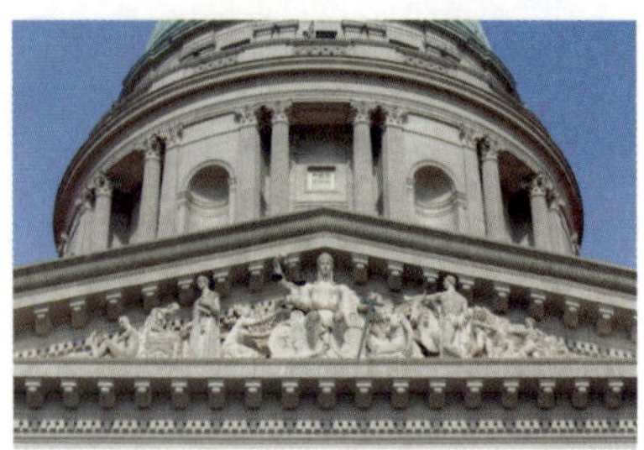

Former Supreme Court's Tympanum, now part of National Gallery Singapore. © National Gallery with Darren Soh.

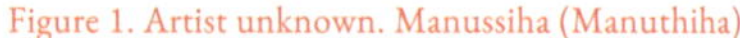

¹ Cited from the artist's proposal submitted for the commission.

Figure 1. Artist unknown. Manussiha (Manuthiha)

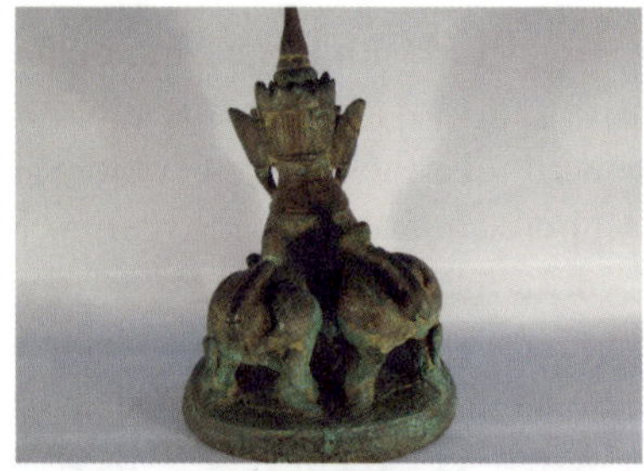

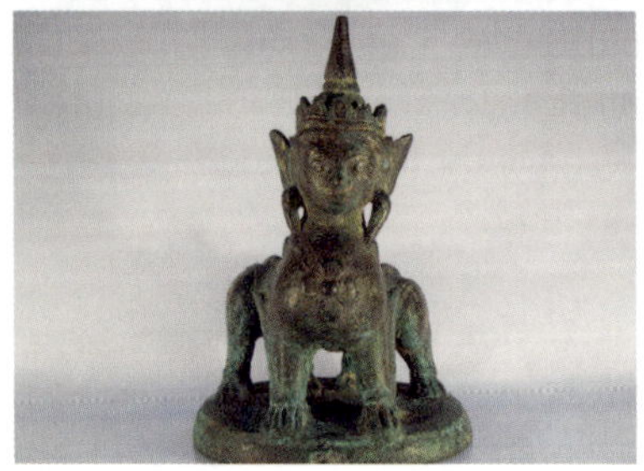

in combat within an arena. Such clashes typically involve each wrestler trying to gain the upper hand in a zero-sum game, where the outcome crowns one party as the victor and the other as the defeated. It is not without significance that Gupta's inflatable sculpture stands as a visual pivot between two Supreme Court buildings: the former Court, now the Gallery, with its neoclassical copper-green dome and the current Court with its glass-paned disc-shaped top. The sculpture's legs point towards the rule of law that undergirds Singapore society, underscoring that no one is above it. The two tussling bodies that converge are not unlike the scales held by the allegorical figure of Lady Justice, prominently displayed on the former Supreme Court's tympanum. It symbolises fairness and objectivity, weighing facts and evidence to arrive at a verdict, thereby restoring balance to society. Gupta intended *Untitled* (2023) as a response to the characteristics of the Gallery's Roof Garden, surrounded by the "visual density of a large metropolis, echoing manufactured realities of global cities."[1]

In this politely laconic sentence, a hint emerges. The reality and history of Singapore required a heavy-handed social contract. This contract has been instrumental in fostering its peace and prosperity, overcoming racial, religious and class differences from the country's colonial era to its independence and now to its status as a capitalistic global city. This rule of law, more often than not, implies the enactment of retributive justice, the restoration of justice through punitive measures, where there is usually an entity or person triumphing in a case enforced through legislation. What is less seen is the performance of restorative justice, where pronouncements aim to reaffirm shared values in a consensual process, recognising the potential for change and reform.

In this contemporary period, statues in the West commemorating the exploits of colonial figures have been vividly toppled in public protest acts against the violence of colonialism and slavery. Such demonstrations are viewed as ethical practices of decolonisation—a refusal to whitewash the past. The search for other ways to occupy public spaces with new forms and symbols to create more historically conscious memories and equitable narratives has become the task at hand. Gupta's inflatable sculpture sits solidly on the deck, drawing up recollections of classical or traditional aesthetic styles in Asia. It brings to mind images like the apotropaic Manussiha guardian statues in Myanmar that possess a human head atop two lion bodies, but more apropos, it also addresses the complexities of the present world order, where contending superpowers are vying for control (or "protection") of the popular imagination. The containment of evil remains elusive.

The head of *Untitled* (2023), bearing the sculpture's weight, displays the human features of two eyes and a nose, but not a mouth. Considering that Gupta's practice often revolves around words—in poetry and other texts—the absence of the mouth, a primary organ for speech, is striking. It appears to remind us that there is a cost either way—of keeping silent and perpetuating, condoning injustice, or of saying too much, speaking out and then facing suppression. What people say or promise also come under scrutiny—will they "walk the talk"? Yet calling out actions, organisations or individuals to expose inequities takes courage because of potential repercussions and harm to the speaker, regardless of whether the words are believed or disbelieved. And what of the eyes? Are the eyes perceived as open or shut? What do they see? And if the inflatable had ears, would they listen instead of merely hearing?

These observations continue themes seen in Gupta's earlier works, such as her series of photographs, performances and sculptures related to *Don't See, Don't Hear, Don't Speak* from 2006 to the present. The artist takes on the popular Gandhian principle of "see no evil, hear no evil, speak no evil", held as a founding national tenet of non-violence in India by literalising the covering up of one's and another's eyes, ears or mouth with our hands (akin to the pictorial maxim of the three wise monkeys). Against the backdrop of ongoing sectarian strife and social rupture since the Partition in 1947, Mahatma Gandhi's aspiration takes a perverse turn in Gupta's works, whereby each individual becomes complicit in the oppression or censorship of the other. And as she depicts children engaging in this mutual sensory restraint, the artist shows how such censoriousness can be internalised and transmitted across generations, leading to reluctance and then stasis. In this context, we aid and abet the political system in evading the truth, all in the name of self and societal preservation. As Shanay Jhaveri writes of Gupta's series:

> It is an envisagement of a dictate to conform, the implication being that the roots of antisocial behaviour stem from a curtailment of agency, an enforcement to kowtow. There is a prevention of individuation, and a call to dehumanizing alienation. The use of children is especially significant; it intimates that such repression is self-perpetuating and transmitted generationally. A visualization of the long lines and chains of repression that begin in childhood, seethe through time and eventually implode. To contest the almost insistent nature of such a drive towards conformity, Gupta has taken her inversion of the Gandhian march literally to the streets

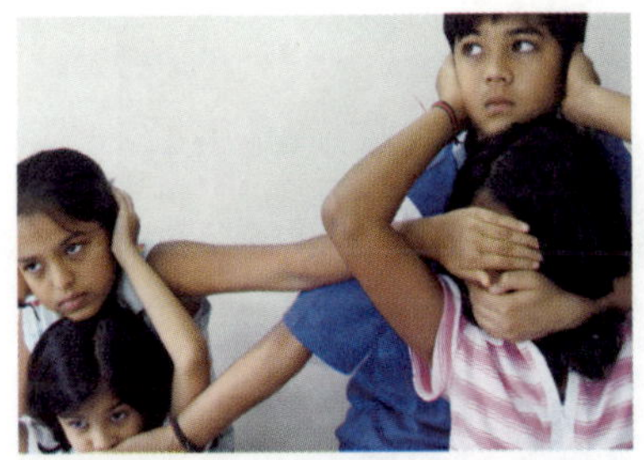

Figure 2. *Untitled (Don't See, Don't Hear, Don't Speak)*

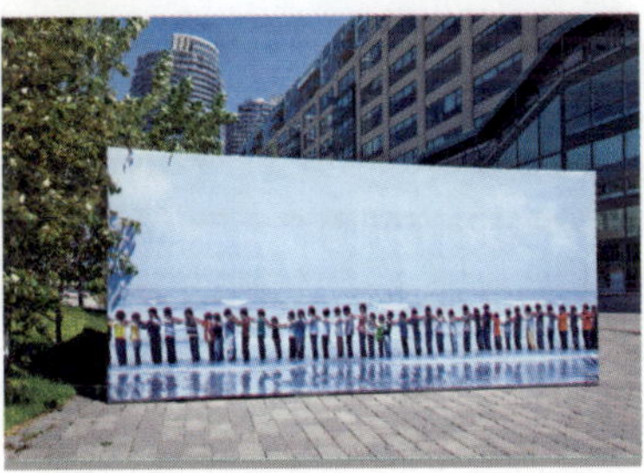

Figure 3. *Untitled (Don't See, Don't Hear, Don't Speak)*

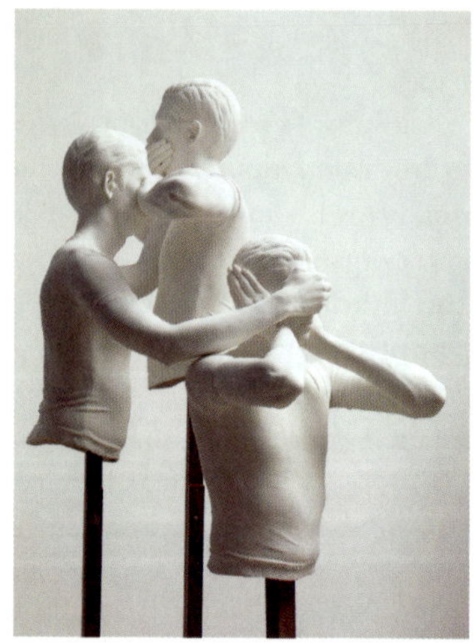

Figure 4. *Untitled (Don't See, Don't Hear, Don't Speak)*

[2] Shanay Jhaveri, "To See Again and Again," In *Shilpa Gupta*, ed. Nancy Adajania (Munich, Berlin, London, New York: Prestel and New Delhi: Vadehra Art Gallery, 2009), 67 and 72.

of various cities. She has organized public performances, most conspicuously in Dubai where groups of individuals were found to be engaged at street corners, on manmade beaches in front of six-star hotels, on the escalators of malls and at fast food chain restaurants in this routine of programmed repression. Billboards in Bolzano, generally used to entice mindless consumption, are washed over with these images of mechanical conformity. Each billboard and performance are a point-to-point demonstration, act of sharing and protests against the self-deceiving impulses of a staggeringly sightless community.[2]

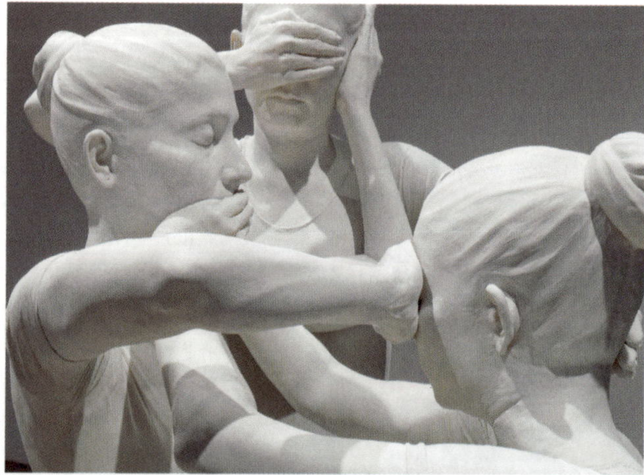

Figure 5. *Untitled (Don't See, Don't Hear, Don't Speak)*

But a reserve of redemptive hopefulness resides within Gupta's inflatable work at the Gallery. The hands that were previously curbing and impeding are now embracing and supporting—the arms on the inflatable cross, one pair clasping the chest on one side, and the other pair in a gripping armlock of solidarity on the other side. This subtle remodeling demonstrates the belief that the vicious cycles of societal conditioning can be broken and that human beings are capable of transcending and transforming their current predicaments.

THREE. (Torso)

Although *Untitled* (2023) finds its origin in a sporting image, Gupta is intrigued by "the seduction and charm in aggressive posturing" exhibited by these figures. These figures proliferate and persist as archetypal or one-dimensional stories of valorous battles and fights in our history books, comics and online games.[3] The set-up of the inflatable on the deck beckons to the young, inviting them into performances of play and

[3] Cited from the artist's proposal submitted for the commission.

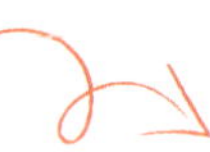

navigation around the spaces created by the entangled vinyl bodies. The artwork's clean lines and indelible form also make it suitable for use as an avatar in video games, transplanting the tactile physicality of the inflatable into a virtual domain, allowing young players to indulge and interact with other online gaming communities. Yet, the artist is also seeking to tease out the undertow of violence and aggression. Accompanying the sculpture on the deck, Gupta also proposes discursive suggestions to explore the topic of play, gaming and warfare through panel talks and workshops for the public. The persistence of aggression narratives in images and storytelling—from history paintings, cartoons, graphic novels or videogame visualisations— would be subjected to expert explication, unpacking and mapping by scholars and psychologists, coming to an understanding of their enduring allure over us.

Ordinarily, game playing would elicit feelings of pleasure and leisure, but increasingly players are inducted into online communities that continue to perpetuate offline hate and divisiveness. Extremist views such as anti-Semitism, racism, homophobia are often found on virtual platforms. Users engage with popular games such as *Call of Duty* and *Minecraft*, and once hooked, they are diverted to private chat channels that operate beyond the reach of moderation, with the greater worry of facilitating the spread of extremist narratives and violent intents amongst public conversations, potentially leading to radicalisation of youths and the propagation of sectarian hate crimes.[4] Often, disenfranchised, alienated individuals are the most vulnerable to such persuasions and persecutions, leading to deeply polarised politics and societal schisms. Games and sports have often been played within the realm of competition, where there are lines of defence demarcating territorial boundaries. In our anxious geopolitical climate, thinking about territory as a form of ultranationalism can quickly lead towards terror and terrorism. Lines, boundaries, borders and barriers are constant presences in Gupta's work, whether visible or invisible. Unlike her initial clay maquette, for *Untitled* (2023), the inflatable is held together by many seams to articulate its body. These lines, although are visually smoothed over when seen from afar, are completely visible up close, and if treated with carelessness, can easily come undone.

In fact, *Untitled* (2023) shares affinities with another body of public light installations that Gupta has made, playing with the senses of being simultaneously familiar (or familial) and yet foreign, "othered". Her works such as *I live under your sky too* (2004–ongoing), *WheredoIendandyoubegin* (2012) and *Deep below, the sky flows under your feet* (2016–17) speak to the impossibility or folly of neat bodily and linguistic divisions, while emphasising the capacious commonality of the sky that is our human firmament.[5] Since 2008, Gupta has derived

4 Carl Miller and Shiroma Silva, "Extremists using video-game chats to spread hate," BBC News, https://www.bbc.com/news/technology-58600181 (accessed 20 June 2023).

5 Anushuka Rajendran, "WheredoIendandyoubegin: Shilpa Gupta's Art of Encounter, Engagement, and Embodiment," In *Shilpa Gupta: Drawing in the Dark*, ed. Thomas Thiel (Berlin: Hatje Cantz VG, 2021). 202–51.

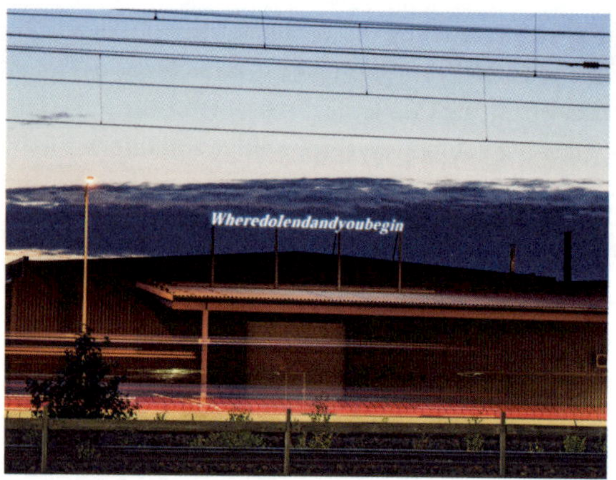 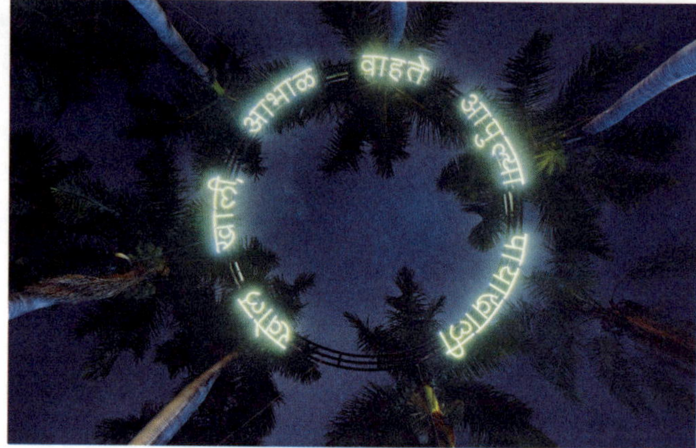

Left: Figure 6. *Wheredolendandyoubegin*

Right: Figure 7. *Deep below, the sky flows under your feet*

new national mappings by superimposing different drawings made by people who were invited to draw outlines of their home countries from memory. She recognises not only the arbitrariness but also the perniciousness of these imagined, paradoxical lines and what they can do to people's identities and daily lives, like asking what happens when another territory resides within another (not unlike how the Tanjong Pagar Railway Station and tracks in Singapore previously had partial Malaysian sovereignty).[6] Like the insubstantial hot air and void within the inflatable, and the immaterial and the contingent in the lighted texts, it is ultimately a futile act to doggedly assume dominance and prevent the inclusion of other possibilities and claimants. The likely outcome of this pursuit is death and destruction.

However, in reinforcing the sensorial tactility and game-like interaction of *Untitled* (2023), Gupta maintains her intentionality and unwavering commitment towards mediated engagements, allowing her viewers to work through their own assumptions, positions or prejudices and achieving understanding and empathy for the Other—a continuity with one another without relinquishing difference. As the Indian feminist-activist writer Urvashi Butalia points out:

> "Each work connects with the one that has gone before and anticipates other associations with those that will come after… she explores what it means to become the other, to cross the borders of identity or to lose that identity and simply be anonymous. … How does the border appear to those on either side of it, to those who manage to cross it, to those who leave it behind and go 'elsewhere', or to someone who may lie on the border's ground and look up at the sky where it does not exist?"[7]

[6] Reuters Staff, "Singapore, Malaysia Agree on Land Swap." Reuters, https://www.reuters.com/article/idINIndia-51608620100920 (accessed 7 June 2023)

[7] Urvashi Butalia. *In Sun at Night.* exh. cat. (London: Ridinghouse and Barbican Centre: 2021). 21–22.

As a free-entry outdoor roof garden commission in an accessible, entertaining medium that is appealing to children and families, the work is consistent with the artist's methodology of going beyond the rarified walls of the museum galleries, improvising with makeshift conditions and having a conversation with participants (who can, at times, take away parts of her work with them). But beyond the dialogue, Gupta is drawn especially to silences and the desire to hold a space for untold stories. She refrains from speaking on behalf, recognising that every time, something is said, something is also left out, of the living and the dead, especially those of women. She asks if it was because these voices were not listened to and therefore did not count.[8]

FOUR. (Psyche)

Much of Gupta's practice has been read through the lens of geopolitical or social struggles, as represented by the two bodies going at each other. *Untitled* (2023) can and will be read in this perspective but it is less obvious that the sensual evocative qualities of the sculptural body have symbolic purchase on references to our internal psychic activities—the emotional split and dualism that we experience in our daily lives. The harm to our physical bodies in combat is coeval with the emotional damage we feel when dealing with conflict and tension. These feelings are sometimes unconsciously expressed through our bodily symptoms (habits, reactions memories, dreams etc.), especially after surviving the fights and dealing with the lingering trauma. Our unconscious is also influenced and shaped by events experienced through our somatic surfaces. Psychoanalytic literature acknowledges the aggressive, conflictual, split, decentralised natures of human beings in modern society and the difficulties of telling ourselves the truth of our desires. This body of literature recognises the repression of knowledge that pervades societal relations partly because we are more moral than we think we are and that morality is actually a repressed desire.[9]

It is productive to read Gupta's roof garden inflatable against another well-known dominant bronze sculpture that is situated at the front of the Gallery next to the City Hall steps—Ng Eng Teng's *Mother and Child* (1996).[10] Both artworks formally feature a central dyad, united yet ultimately separate. Ng's sculpture, which is now in proximity, introduces the unanswered question of gender into Gupta's work, which the latter leaves as enigmatic. As a gendered-female author of this essay, I would invariably identify Gupta's work as a female subject or feminine in its energy, galvanised by the prospect of reading her work with one of Ng's—an established patriarch in Singapore's art history whose sculptures are regarded as archetypal

[8] "Hover, echo, persist: Shilpa Gupta in conversation with Hilary Floe", in ibid, p.38.

[9] John Rajchman, "Lacan and the Ethics of Modernity," *Representations* 15 (1986): 42–56.

[10] Cast in Taiwan and the last monumental work produced by Ng Eng Teng, *Mother and Child* remained in Ng's studio for several years and was temporarily sited at Tampines Central Park before finally moving to the Gallery in 2019, where it was installed on the existing pavement structure in front of the Gallery, becoming part of its façade that faces the Padang. Another work of the same title and produced in 1980 is located at Orchard Parade Hotel.

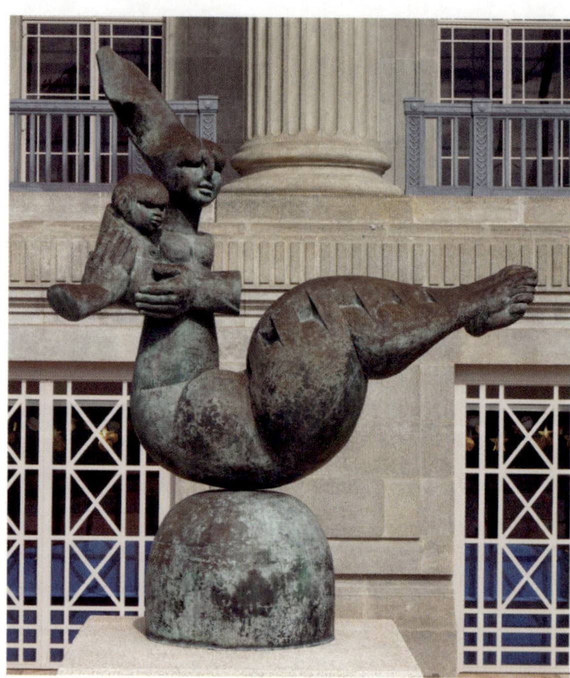

representations of maternal love. However, there is much more interpretive and psychical complexity than meets the eye.[11]

Ng's oeuvre dealt primarily with the figure and the human condition. His philosophy was grounded in the belief that humanity began with the family where children would learn values through the dynamic relationships with their parents. The recurrent motif of "mother and child" through various compositions in his body of works, articulates the supportive role that a mother plays in her offspring's life. His sculptures portray the child sitting restfully on the mother's lap or in her embracing arms. In this particular work, the mother's large, disembodied hands appear to be protectively pressing her child close but at the same time, they seem to be trying to put the child aside, separating the child from herself and insisting on a difference, sometimes an opposition. This is also observed by T.K. Sabapathy who perceptively notes that:

> "The children or child for example even as it is dependent it is also asserting a sense of individuality, asserting a presence either to get away from or wrapping itself around the mother; what emerges are the conditions of duality. On the one hand attentive, and on the other hand looking way. There are tensions, all the time."[12]

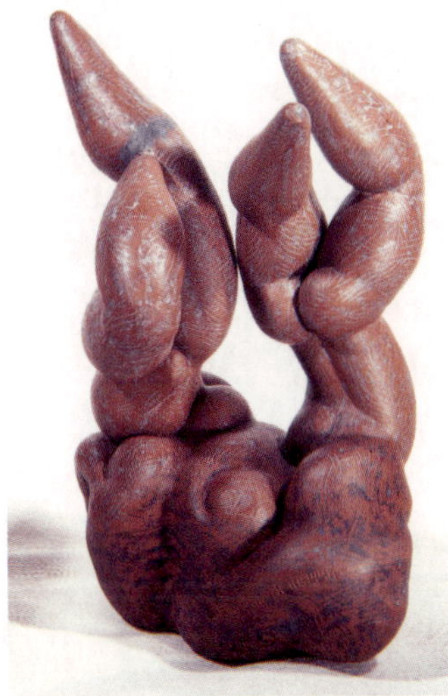

Figure 9. Ng Eng Teng. *Inverted Torsos*

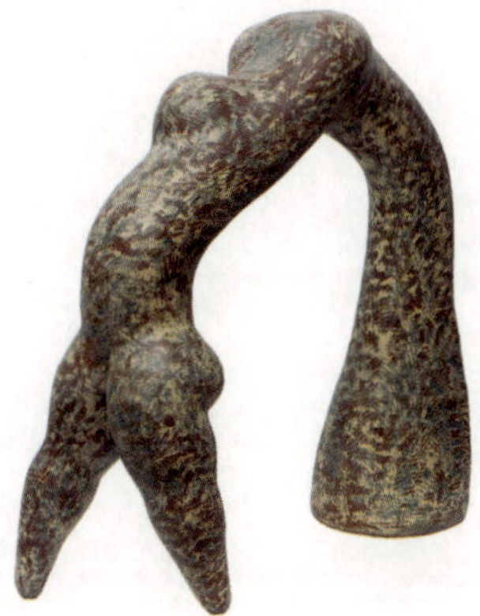

Figure 10. Ng Eng Teng. *Acrobat*

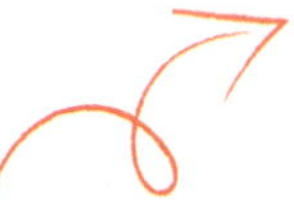

[13]Audre Lorde, *A Burst of Light and Other Essays*, (Mineola, New York: Ixia Press, 2017), 95. Originally published 1988 by Firebrand Books (Ithaca, NY).

Uncanny relations can also be drawn between Gupta's *Untitled* (2023) and Ng's other late works from the 1990s, such as *Inverted Torsos* (1994) and *Acrobat* (1994), with the forms expressing emergent fluid shapes that appear almost falling over or bending over backwards—behavioural metaphors not lost on parents.[13] These sculptures relate again to his works in the 1970s with rockers and stabiles that are grounded in the principle of tension. The figures can roll around without being toppled over, acting as images of resilience in the midst of personal struggles.

In this regard, it does feel as if Gupta's *Untitled* (2023) is speaking in concert with Ng's *Mother and Child* (1996), addressing me as a woman—a potential or thwarted maternal figure but equally a child to a mother—asking us collectively how we might set aside our egos, hold ambiguities, ambivalences, contradictions together and in balance. Could we not neglect our communing bodies and independent minds despite being torn between our obligations? Could we not instead dance, legs in the air, head over heels, with splits and headstands, and with utter clarity of thought despite the blood rushing to our heads? What are the lessons here?

Gupta's sculpture exudes honesty and fortitude, a forcefully quiet grace. As her work shows me, I am capable of allowing movement and transformation because I am firmly grounded and supported. The arms holding her inflatable bodies together are those of compassion, radiating the radical self-care that the then cancer-stricken feminist writer-activist Audre Lorde once exhorted: "Caring for myself is not self-indulgence, it is self-preservation, and that is an act of political warfare." Lorde had to reconcile differences within herself, from a healthy body she once knew and accept the challenge of discerning the distinction between overextension and not stretching oneself to one's capabilities. It was necessary for her to tell the difference—"Crucial. Physically. Psychically."[13]

Dr **Adele Tan** received her PhD in art history from The Courtauld Institute of Art, University of London and is currently Senior Curator at National Gallery Singapore. Her research focuses on modern and contemporary art in Southeast Asia and China. Her recent projects include the exhibition *Awakenings: Art in Society in Asia, 1960s to 1990s*, the 2019 annual Ng Teng Fong Roof Garden Commission with the artist Charles Lim Yi Yong, and *OUTBOUND*, a series of large-scale site-specific artwork commissions at the Gallery. She completed a monographic exhibition on Singapore artist Lin Hsin Hsin (2021) and will be working on upcoming exhibitions on Singapore-born British artist Kim Lim (2024) and the revamp of the DBS Singapore Gallery (2025).

ART AND A PSYCHIATRIST

PROF. CHONG SIOW ANN, GUEST CONTRIBUTOR

We are now living in a world that is fraught with injustices, conflicts, calamities and looming threats to our climate and environment. We seem to be failing in our stewardship of the planet and messing things up for the generations to come. Amidst this chaotic time of anomie, mistrust, paranoia and ruptures, artists are creating provocative and evocative artworks in response to these upheavals. Galleries and art museums are conjoined in these endeavours. They have long been instrumental in shaping public discourse, increasing awareness, educating and influencing community attitudes, and reflecting the values of the communities they serve.

In the similar vein, National Gallery Singapore has commissioned a work by Shilpa Gupta, an Indian contemporary artist internationally known for her works that explore issues of the nation state, identity, religion, technology and the human condition.

When I was asked to write an essay on this artwork, I felt some trepidation. Being a non-expert, what could I say that wouldn't fall short of the topic and who am I to speak of it?

As a psychiatrist without any formal qualifications in art, I have nonetheless had the good fortune of having memorable experiences with art in its various forms—all of which had an intense and profound effect on me. They have compelled me to reflect, to learn more about what I have seen and felt and to seek for more of these aesthetic experiences.

Art stimulates our senses and emotions and it goes beyond mere entertainment that just amuses us. Art clarifies our perceptions, uncovering thoughts that were previously unknown to us and increasing our awareness of the complexities in our life and the wider world that might otherwise be hidden, overlooked or denied. It has certainly played an important role in my personal and professional life by igniting my imagination, enriching my sensibilities, and making me (I hope) a more thoughtful and sensitive doctor.

It was, after all, a psychiatrist who had written of the concept of "ideational mimetics." Sigmund Freud, widely acknowledged as the father of psychoanalysis, posited that original artwork offers an exchange of energy between the viewer and the art. Experiencing art is not just sensory stimulation but also an emotional and intellectual endeavour. When people project their emotions, ideas and/or memories onto objects, they enact a process similar to empathy—which according to Freud, is necessary not only for the practice of psychoanalysis, but essential for the functioning and maintenance of any civilised society. Interacting with art is, hence, humanising.

Having committed myself to this writing project, I'd decided to begin with a Freudian aesthetic approach, starting with the artist herself.

When I spoke to Shilpa Gupta via a video-call, she was at her home in Mumbai, India. Born and raised there, she grew up within the fold of a large multi-generational family. "There is always a lot going on," Gupta said of her close-knit family, and from whom she learned "to say what you want to say without breaking ties."

Despite growing up as a woman in a traditional and conservative South Asian society and having to juggle her professional and domestic responsibilities (she is also the mother of an 11-year-old boy), which she wryly commented that it often meant "multi-tasking to a hysterical level", she possesses a calm confidence of someone who goes her own way.

As a child who excelled at her studies, she inevitably carried the weight of parental expectations and initially—and rather conventionally—studied computer science in high school and later in a science college. However, she soon found it to be too restrictive for her to explore the complexities of life. She "fought" to leave her science college despite the concerns of her parents and the college principal; at the age of 16, she enrolled in the Sir Jamsetjee Jeejeebhoy School of Art in Mumbai.

During her first year in the School of Art in 1992, a mob of Hindu nationalists tore down the Babri Masjid, a 16th-century mosque built by the Muslim Mughals. In the riots that followed, thousands of people, mostly Muslims, were killed across India, igniting retaliatory violence with serial bombings in Mumbai.[1] She remembers hearing bomb blasts while travelling home from school. The horrors of the slaughter unleashed by religious fundamentalism and the fear and suspicion that spread thereon sparked her art activism.

Over the last two and a half decades, Gupta has used various mediums including sculpture, photography, text, sound, light and ephemera to interrogate and make visible issues of oafish nationalism, oppressive state apparatus, divisive social and gender identity politics, class barriers and their degrading effects on individuals and societies.

So much of who we are and what we do with our lives are rooted in our distant past and Gupta's artistic journey and her works have grown organically from the loam of her native soil. Her upbringing and personal experiences in the context of complex Indian politics have made her an inquisitive challenger of the status quo and a believer of transcending borders and dissolving boundaries.

The French-American artist, Louise Bourgeois, once said, "Something is a work of art when it has filled its role as therapy for the artist. I don't care about the audience. I'm not working for the audience."[2] In sharp contrast, Gupta's art is not self-indulgent. She takes her viewers and their responses into account, endeavouring to have a dialogue with them through her quiet, engaging and minimalist aesthetic.

We can see and feel that aesthetic in the sculpture that she has created for the Gallery. She has deliberately left the work untitled, which I take it to mean that she wants to retain a degree of ambiguity and for us to approach it with an open mind, as if conversing with a stranger who has interesting things to say.

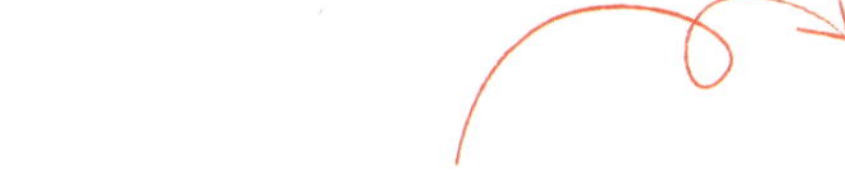

[1] BBC News. "Timeline: Ayodhya holy site crisis." 20 September 2010. n.p.

[2] Amei Wallach. "Is It Art? Is It Good? And Who Says So?" *The New York Times.* 12 October 1997. n.p.

The preeminent and long-time art critic of *The New Yorker* magazine, the late Peter Schjeldahl, once asked this question for which he also offered the answer: "Where could one put outsized works that were almost invariably abstract…to give them a chance of seeming to mean something? In nature!"[3]

And so, it is at the Ng Teng Fong Roof Garden atop National Gallery Singapore where Gupta's imposing three-dimensional semi-abstract inflatable sculpture sits—surrounded by greenery, in sunlight and shade, and with a segment of the cityscape as part of its backdrop.

To create a large sculpture is an act of audacity. It assumes and demands its space in an already crowded world. For it to stake its claim, a sculpture must have immediate, arresting and enduring dramatic effect and a gravitas of its own.

From a distance, Gupta's *Untitled* (2023) is a dark-toned sculpture that looks like a gigantic multi-limbed creature that has come to a sudden halt in mid-stride after tumbling down with its head on the ground. Despite its appearance, the curvy and graceful pose invites you to approach it, touch and feel it.

It reminds me of the immense sculptures of the French American avant-gardist Niki de Saint Phalle that she called *Nanas* (a not too polite French slang for a girl or young saucy woman). The *Nanas* were initially inspired by a pregnant friend of Saint Phalle, and they are large-scaled vibrant voluptuous figures that are hyperbolically feminine, symbolising femininity and maternity. (A feminist, Saint Phalle had said that she enjoyed the thought of men looking "very small" next to her works.)[4]

Gupta's sculpture, however, is androgynous; and walking around it, I find that there is no right vantage point and each step gives a different perspective and configuration. The two bodies are interlocked in a pugilistic position. The viewer immediately senses the intense energy of the four legs flung into the air and the overall sense of combative duality.

Through the eyes of a psychiatrist, Gupta's sculpture strikes me as a visual metaphor for the mind-body dualism that lies at the heart of of my profession. This prompts me to reflect on the origin and history of that schism between brain-based and mind-based psychiatry and its implications on how we think about and approach our state of mind and its disorders.

[3] Peter Schjeldahl. "Returning to Storm King." *The New Yorker*. 24 August 24 2020. https://www.newyorker.com/magazine/2020/08/31/returning-to-storm-king

[4] Peter Schjeldahl. "The Pioneering Feminism of Niki de Saint Phalle." *The New Yorker*. 5 April 2021. https://www.newyorker.com/magazine/2021/04/05/the-pioneering-feminism-of-niki-de-saint-phalle

The enduring conundrum of whether mental illnesses stem from brain abnormalities or the mind can be traced back to the work of the 17th-century philosopher René Descartes. Descartes advocated the idea that mind and body were separate entities, with mental activity originating from a substance distinct from the body (an idea now commonly referred to as 'Cartesian dualism').

In the late 19th to early 20th century, researchers explored the brain's anatomy to identify the origins of mental disorders. However, when these studies ultimately proved fruitless, their failure led to a split in the field. Freudian psychoanalysis, with its emphasis on conflicts in the unconscious, began to take precedence over the biological camp. Despite lacking scientific evidence to back their theories and practices, this mind-based, non-biological analytic camp became the influential force in psychiatry. However, that changed with the subsequent discoveries of efficacious drugs for some serious mental illnesses in the mid-twentieth century. The suggestion that chemical imbalances and aberrant brain circuits could explain mental illness and that it would all be a matter of time before these could be uncovered became tantalising. (The pharmaceutical industry enthusiastically promoted the idea that brain chemistry could provide a pathogenesis for mental illness, offering medications to treat them.) The pendulum swung. This brain-based, biological paradigm became the primary foundation for understanding mental illness, though this "biological revolution", once full of promise, has also now faced some challenges. In the United States (US), the final decade of the twentieth century was declared the 'Decade of the Brain.' However, in 2010, the director of the National Institute of Mental Health in the US reflected that the initiative had not produced any significant increase in recovery rates from mental illness.

Many now feel that the pendulum has swung too far and a purely brain-based approach risks dehumanising psychiatry. Such an approach reduces the patient's illness to an objective neurological explanation, devoid of all the nuances of the individual's social context, emotions, personal values and unique perspective of their condition.

Mental suffering takes many forms and has many contributory causes, only some of which are rooted in brain abnormalities. The reality is that psychiatry is neither 'mindless' nor 'brainless' but involves both; mental illnesses are, in almost all instances, the confluence of the person's biological constitution and other psychosocial factors. On a different level, Gupta's sculpture, at least to me, is also a representation of the multifactorial causes of most mental illnesses: the two battling torsos of the sculpture merge into a single head that houses the most complex and baffling organ.

Just as I relate to this piece through the idiosyncratic channel of my experiences and creation, others would see and feel this piece differently. Some might see it as a visual metaphor of a topsy-turvy world upended by its own makings where the two battling bodies can be read as an allegory of the ongoing geopolitical strife and social struggles. For the younger viewers who are digital natives, the work could also allude to the entangled dualities of their offline and online lives.

And I reckon that is what good abstract art should do. It is complex and demands our attention and efforts to discern our emerging impressions and feelings and decipher them for their meanings and insights, which would vary because of our unique individual sensibility, life experiences and memories.

Art may not be obligated to change our lives, but it often does anyway. A visit to behold and contemplate this sculpture would be a biographical event: from the moment we view this piece to the moment we depart, we could be a different person from who we were before.[5] Regardless, viewing it on the roof of National Gallery Singapore would be, to borrow a fine phrase from Peter Schjeldahl, "a holiday of the spirit on the crowded calendar of life lived."[6]

[5] Hanya Yanagihara. "What Should We Expect of Art?" *The New York Times*. 18 August 2022. n.p.

[6] Peter Schjeldahl. "When a Museum Feels Like Home." *The New Yorker*. 15 & 22 February 2021. https://www.newyorker.com/magazine/2021/02/15/when-a-museum-feels-like-home

---

Professor **Chong Siow Ann** is a distinguished psychiatrist who practises and teaches at the Institute of Mental Health (IMH) in Singapore. Prof. Chong's research interests encompass mental health topics, such as mood disorders, psychosis and dementia. He has been actively involved in various aspects of mental health, including clinical work, research and education, and is well-published in respected medical journals. Prof. Chong also regularly contributes articles to Singapore's leading newspaper, *The Straits Times*, where he discusses mental health-related topics and shares insights from his professional experience.

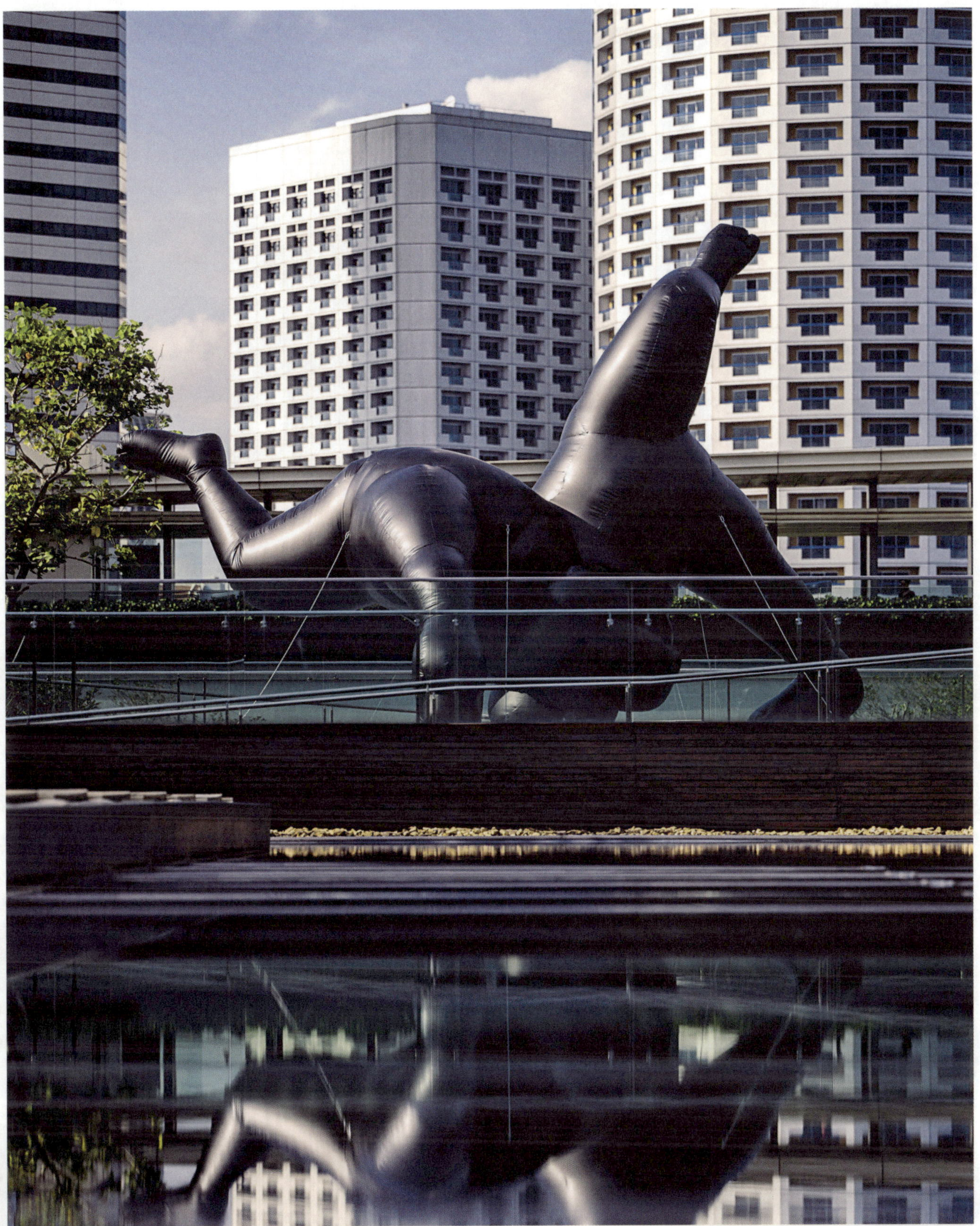

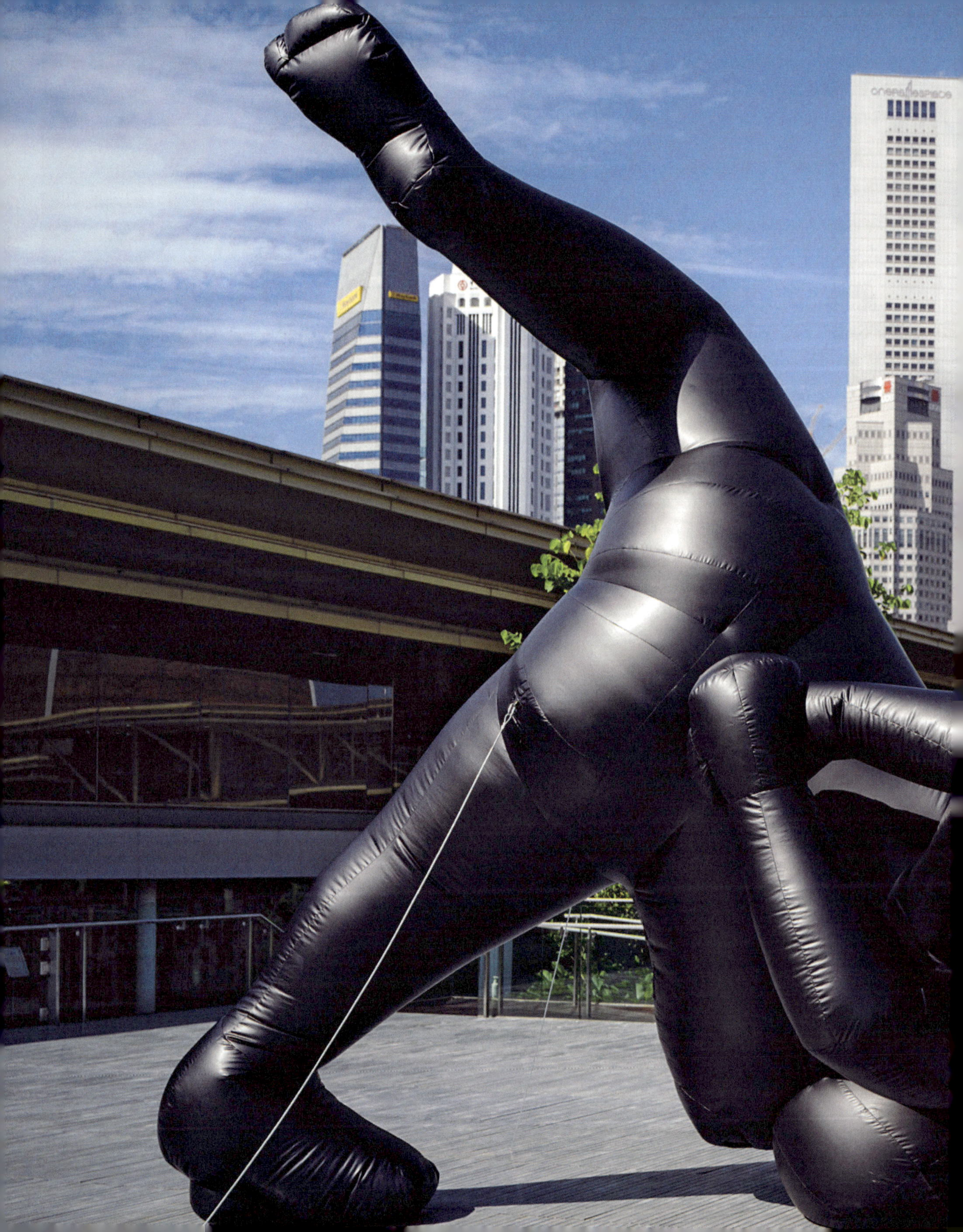

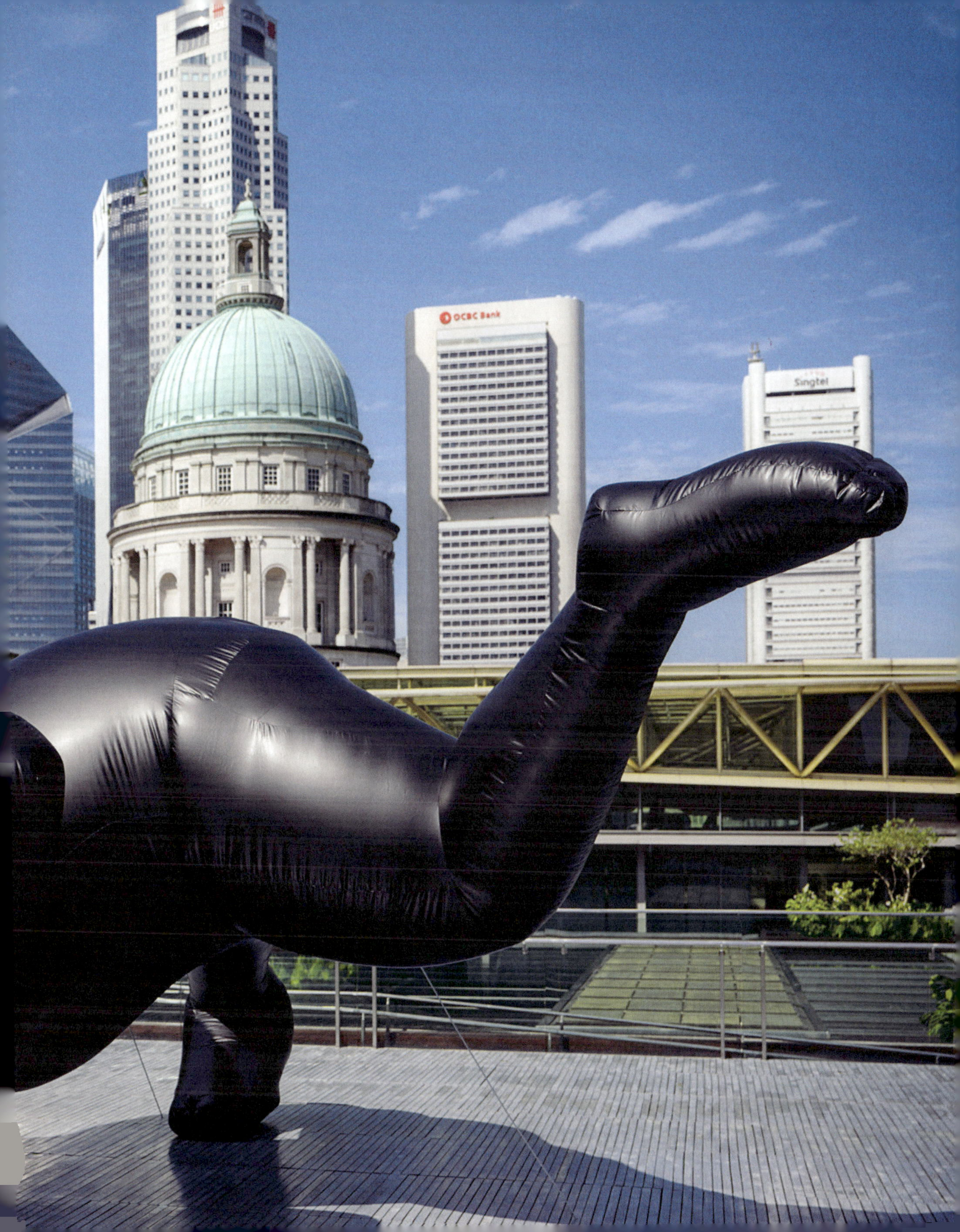

OCBC Bank
Singtel

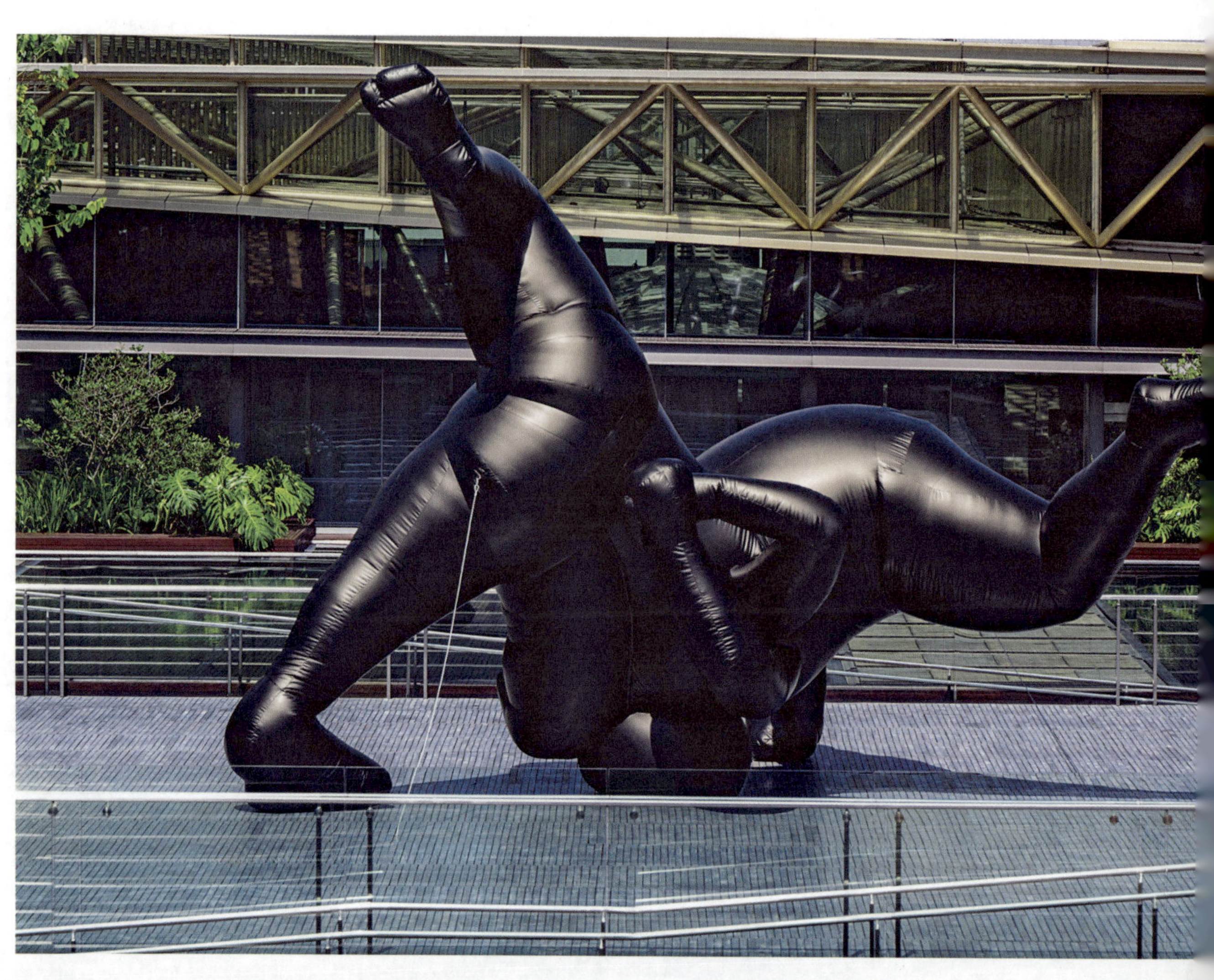

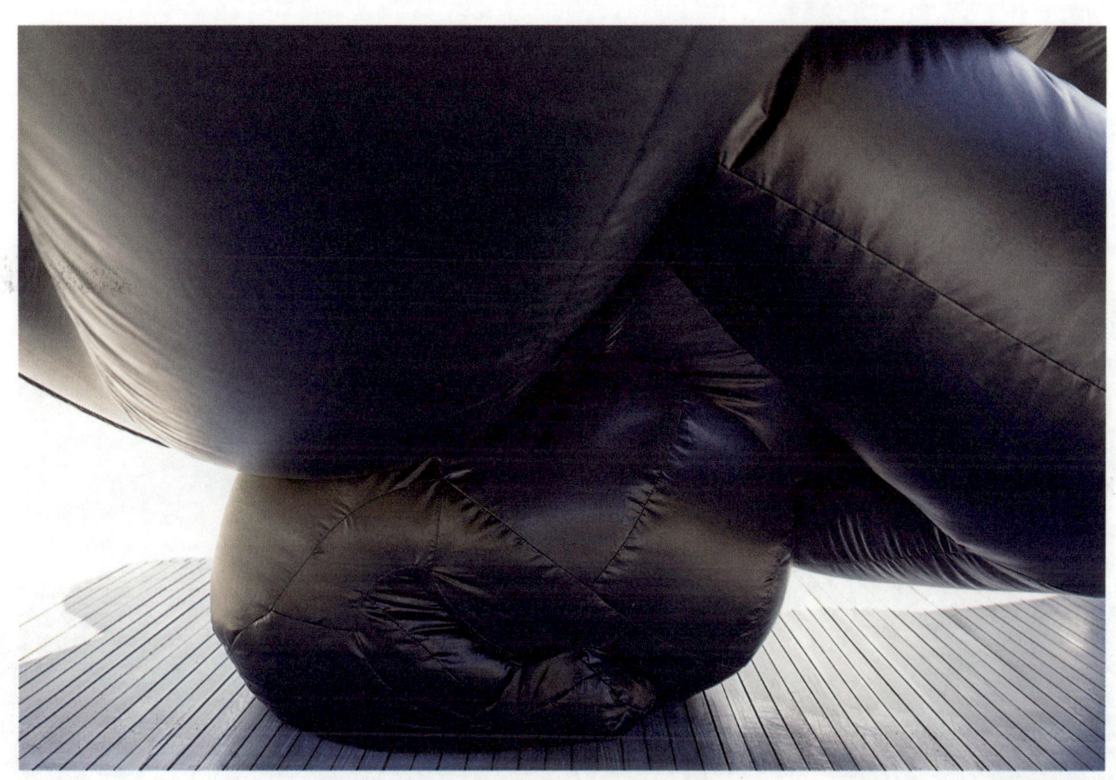

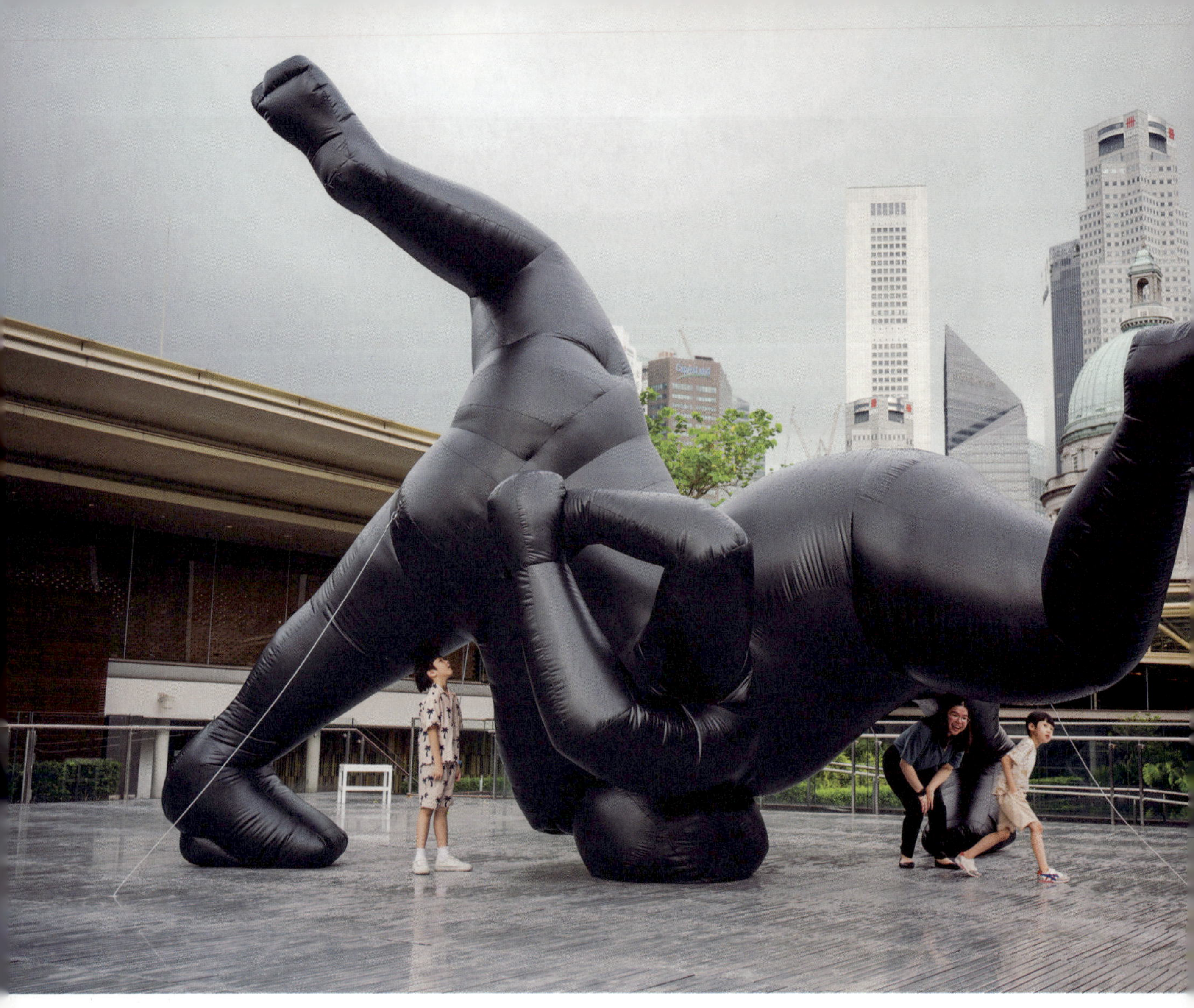

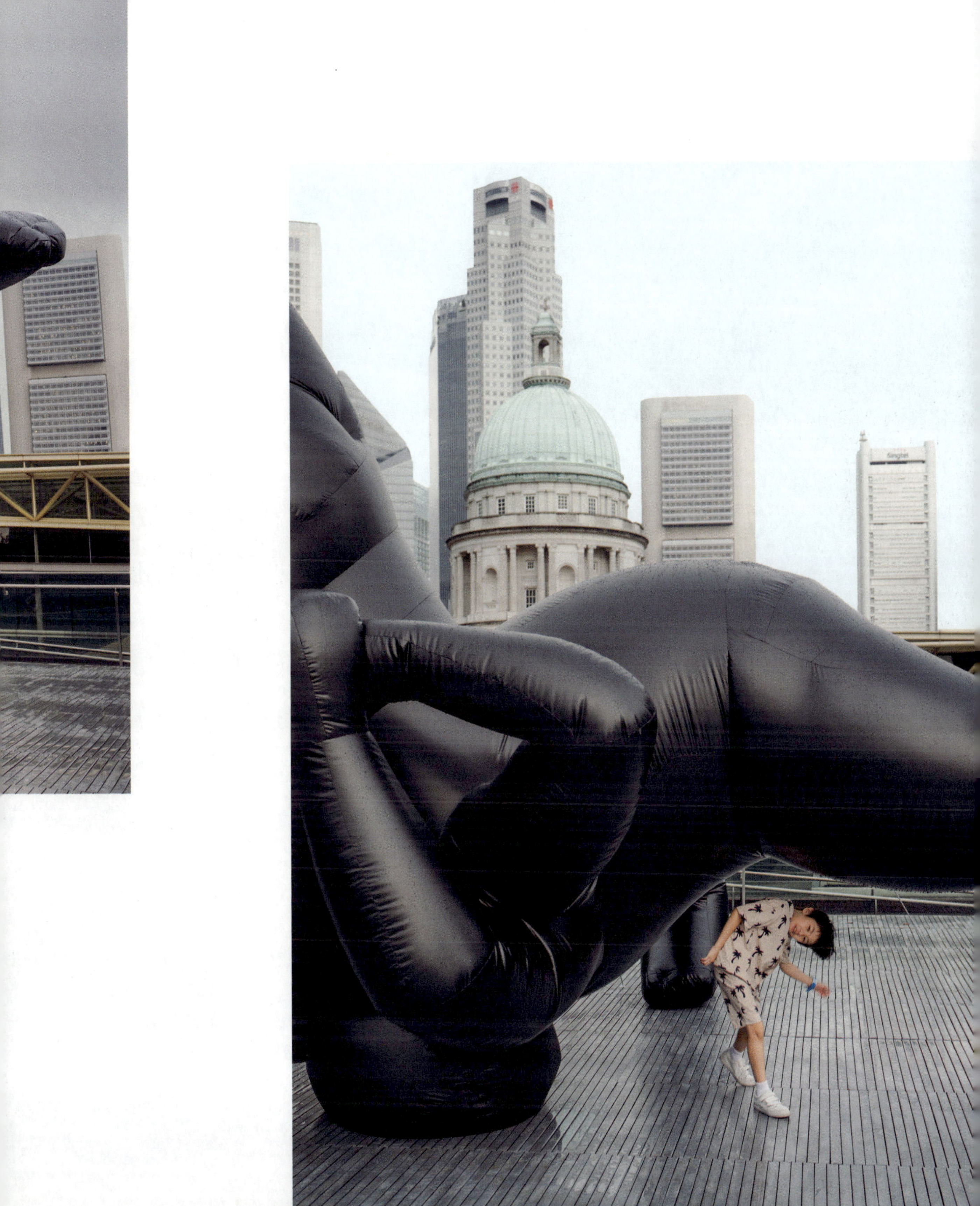

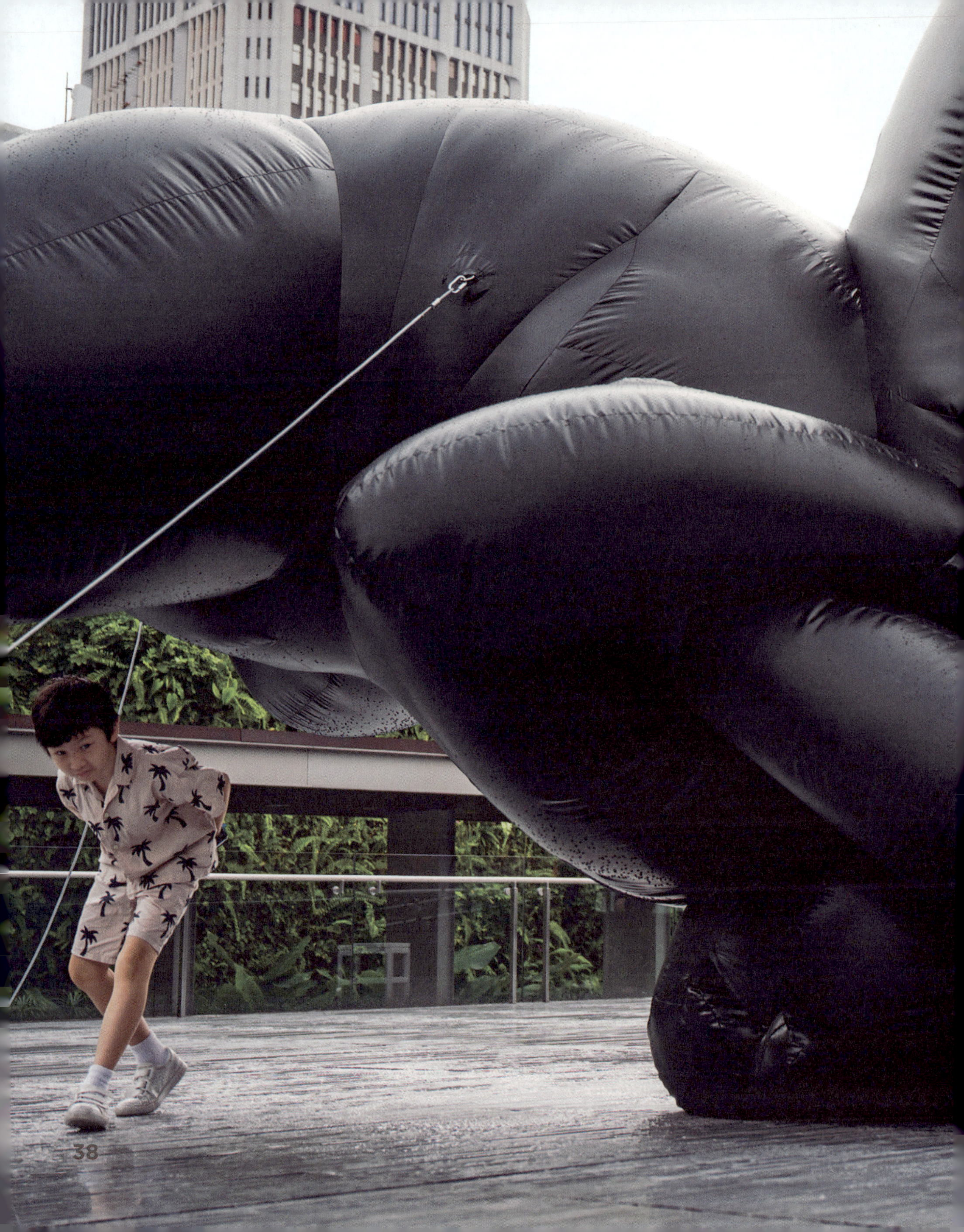

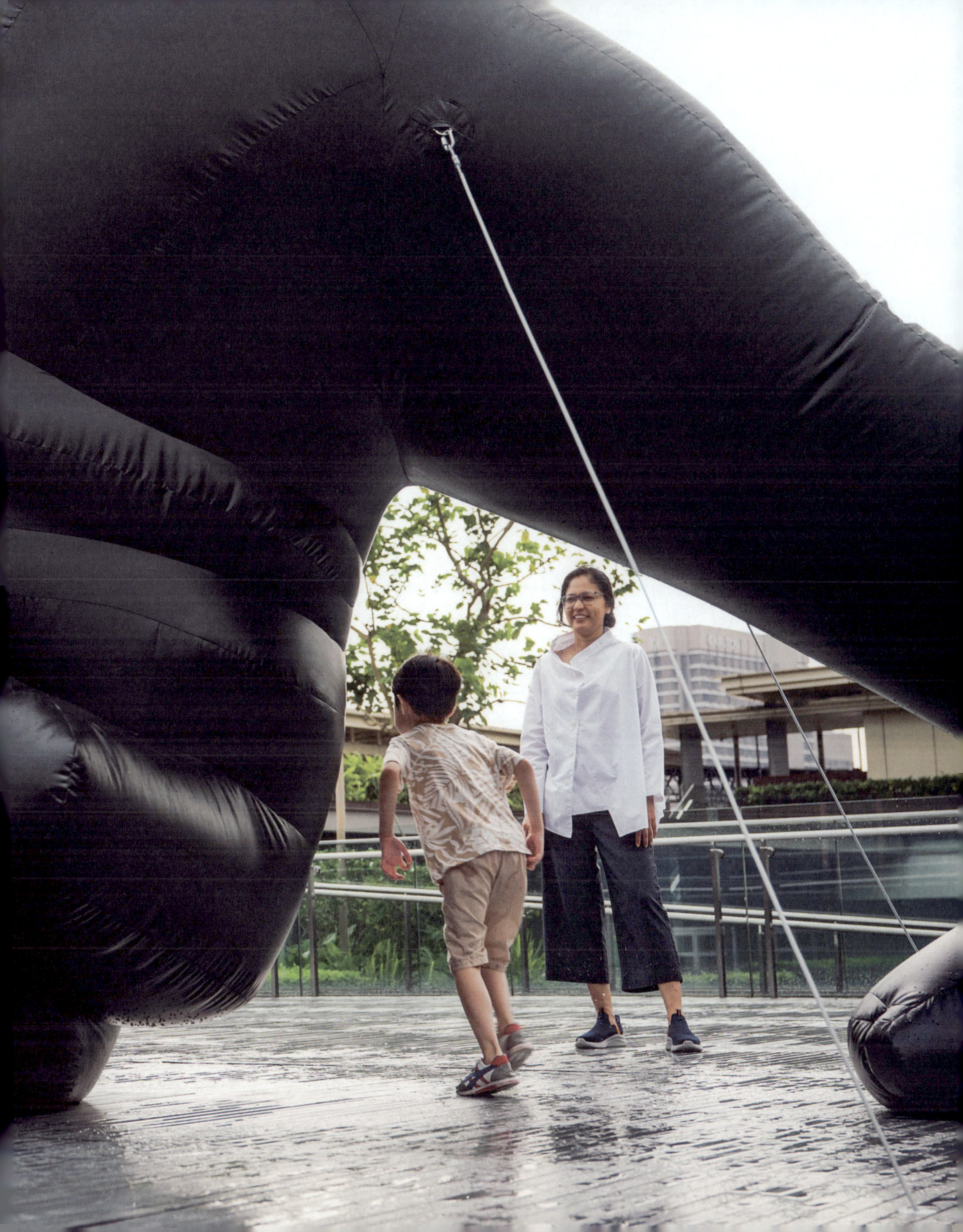

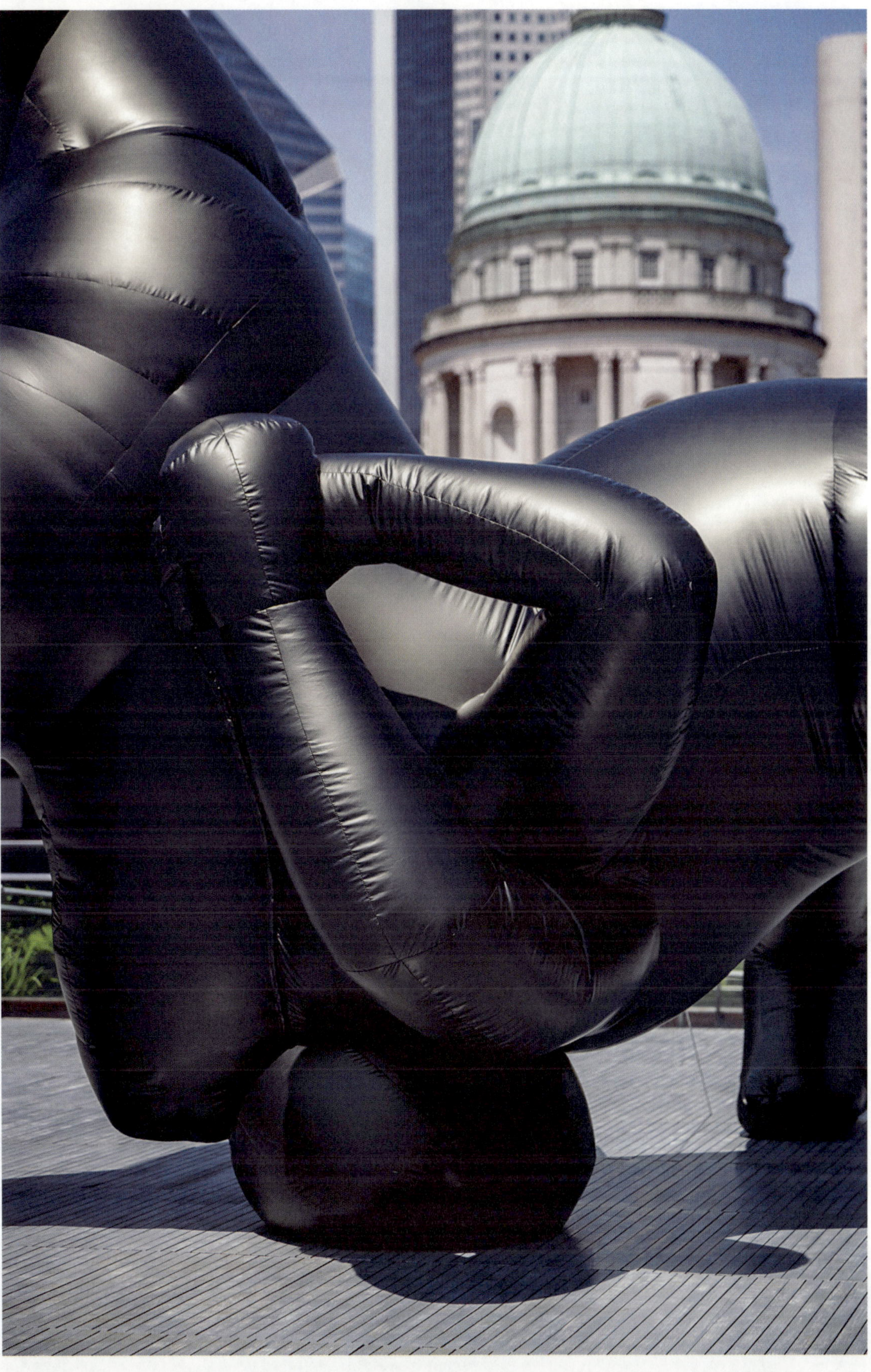

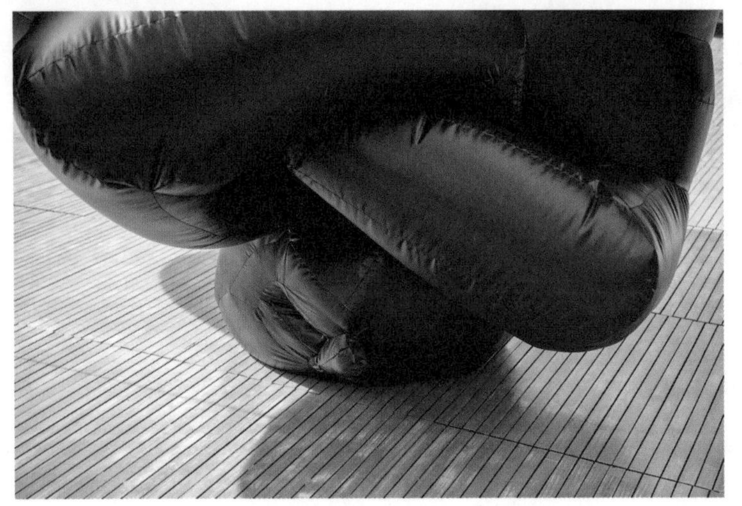

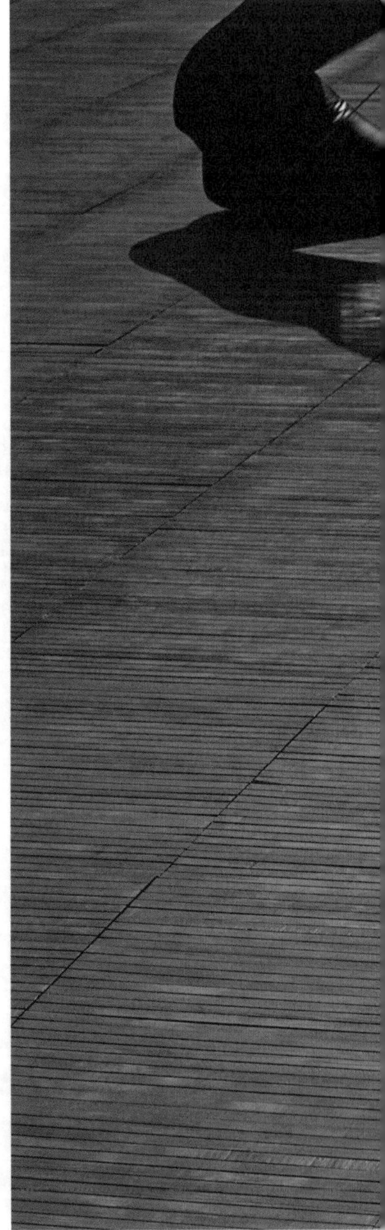

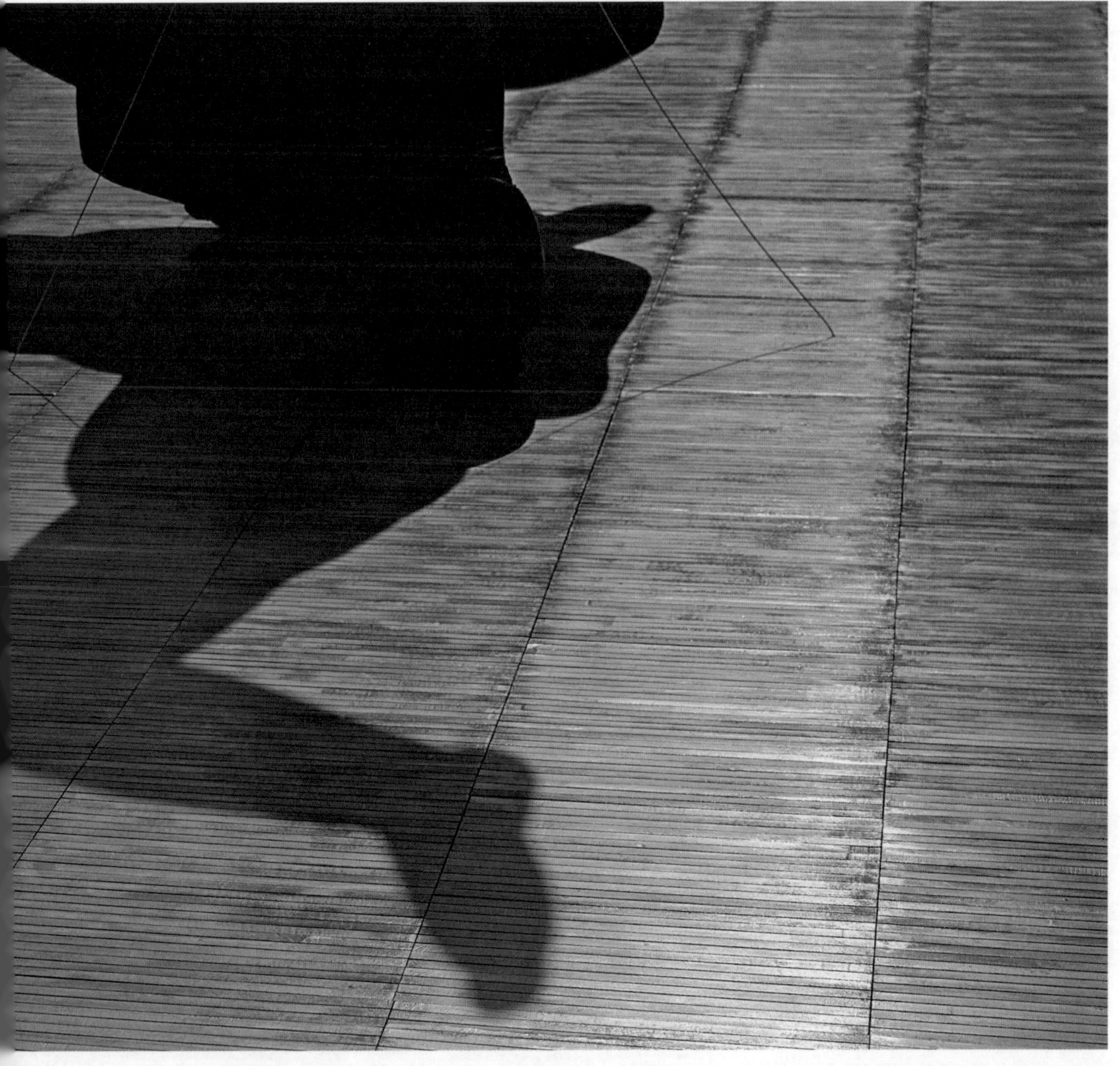

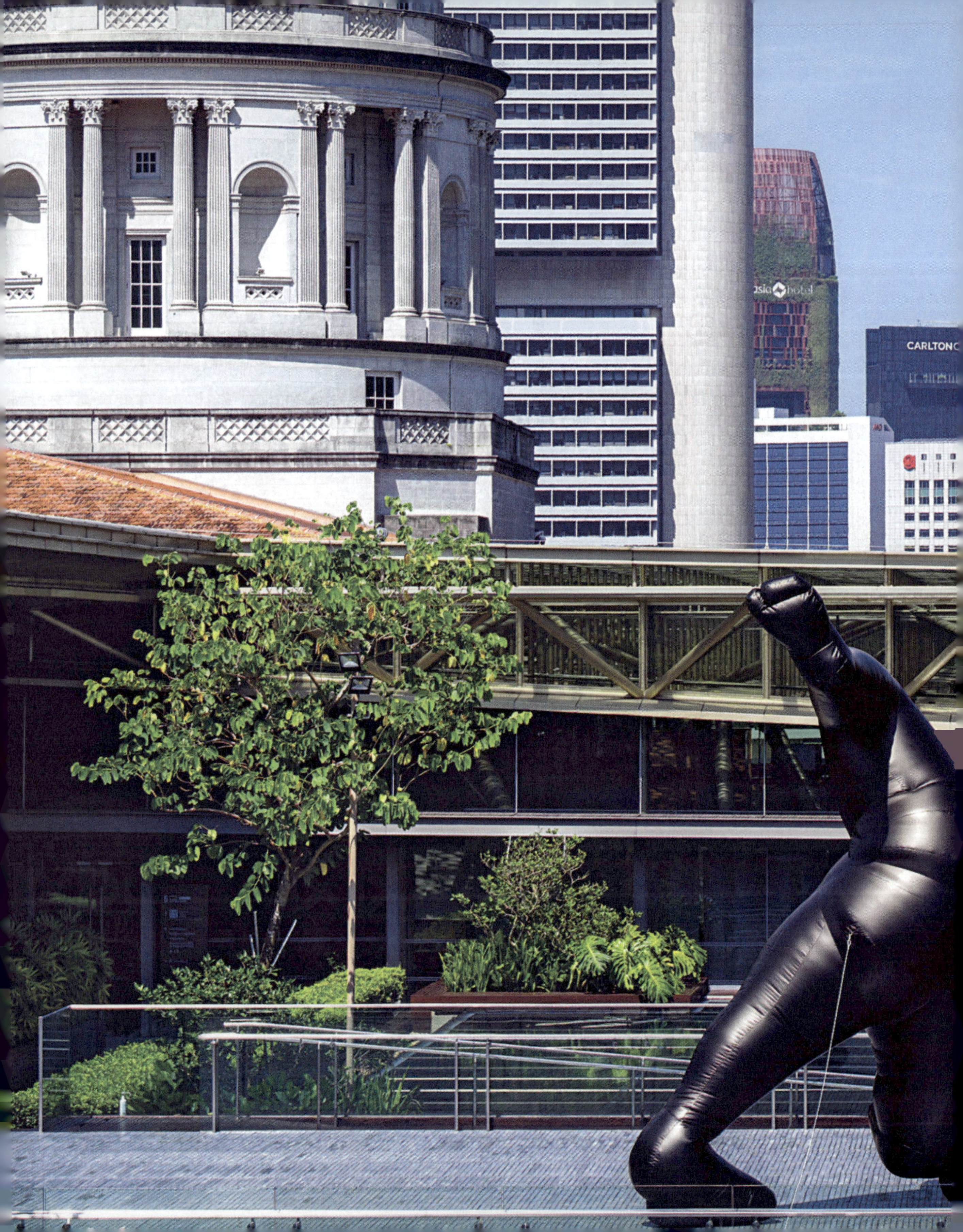

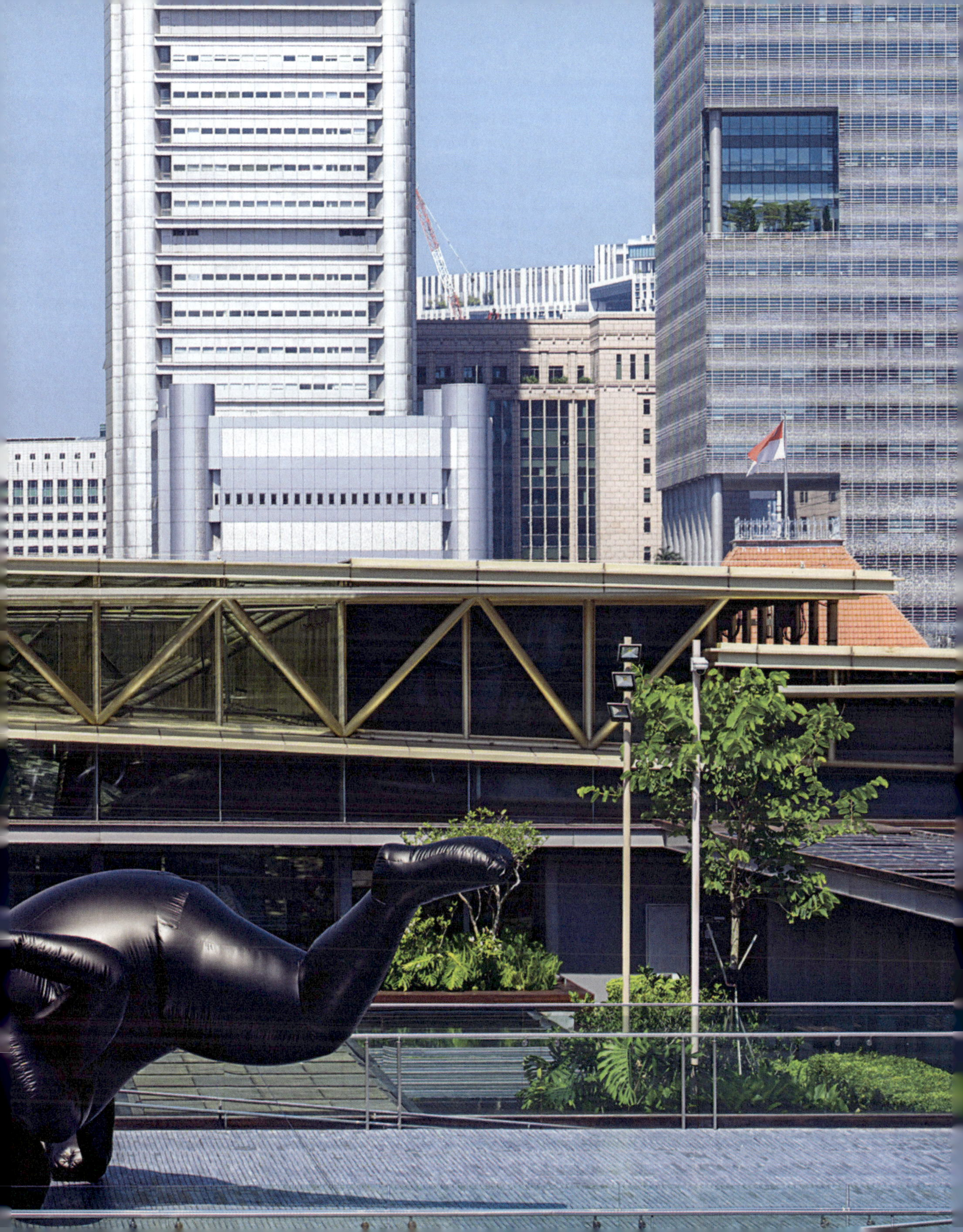

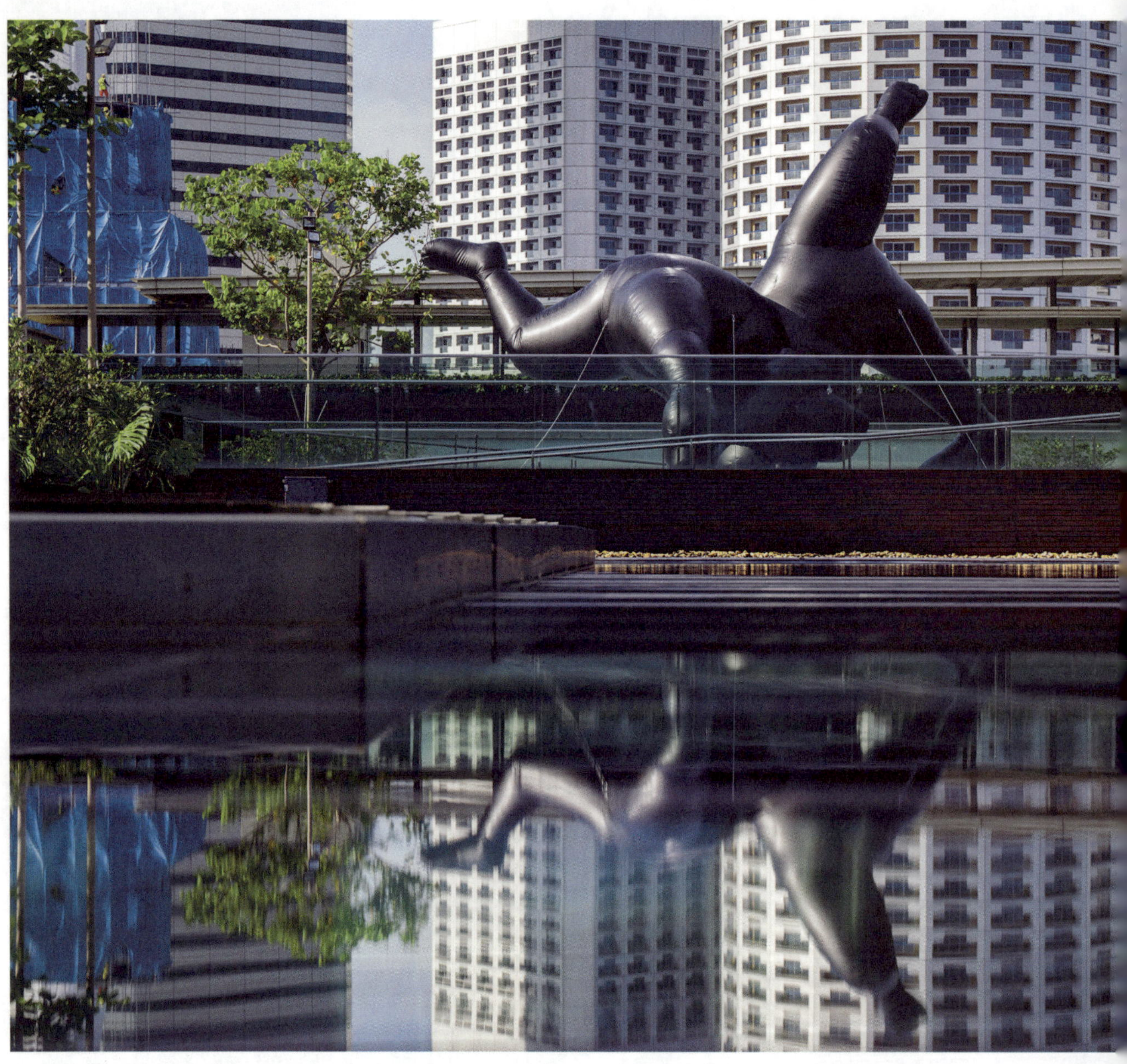

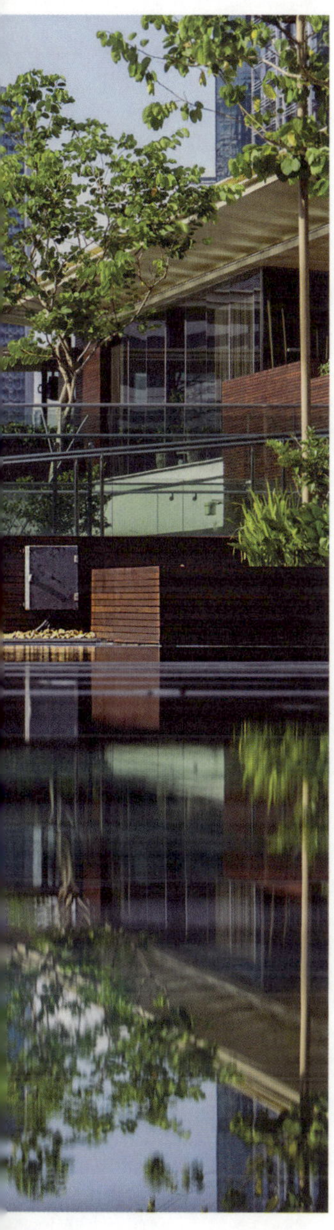

Biography

Shilpa Gupta lives and works in Mumbai, India. Growing up in South Asia has had a significant influence on her work, which often seeks to blur the lines and embrace all the potential meanings that people may read into it. Gupta uses her art to tackle sensitive topics like nationalism and class barriers with subtlety and nuance, creating opportunities for dialogue. Her work is shaped by her interest in research, pedagogy and learning, seeing it as an open-ended and reciprocal dialogue with the communities she interacts with and the public that explores her work.

Gupta's works have been shown in leading international institutions and museums such as Tate Modern, Museum of Modern Art, Louisiana Museum, Centre Pompidou, Serpentine Gallery, Fondazione Sandretto Re Rebaudengo, Mori Museum, Solomon R. Guggenheim Museum, ZKM, Ishara Art Foundation, Kiran Nadar Museum and Devi Art Foundation.

A full list of exhibitions and public works is available on the artist's website: https://shilpagupta.com/

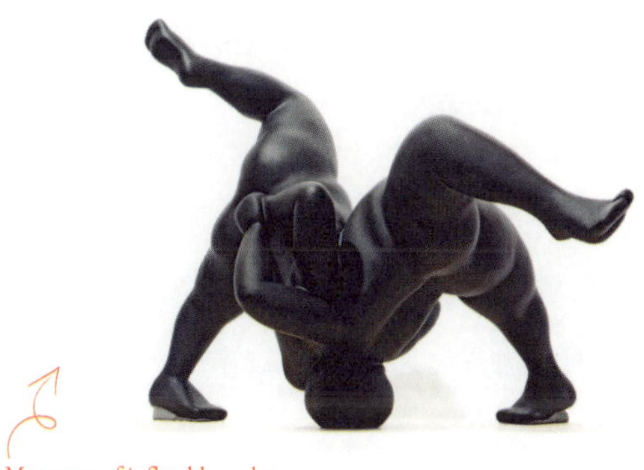

Maquette of inflatable sculpture

List of Illustrations

Acknowledgements

SERIES PARTNER

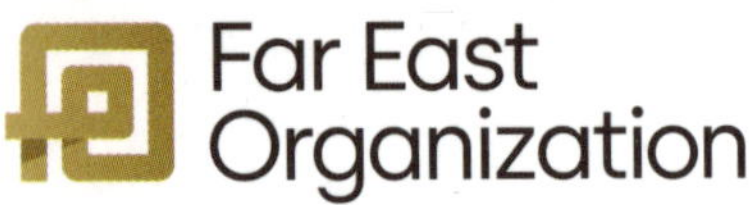

EXHIBITION TEAM

CURATOR
Adele Tan

PROJECT DIRECTOR
Seng Yu Jin

ARTWORK & EXHIBITION MANAGEMENT
See Jia Jun
Benedict Tan
Teo Yen Sy

EXHIBITION FABRICATION
SPACElogic Pte Ltd

COMMUNITY & ACCESS
Jocelyn Ang
Januavi Lee
Alicia Teng
and all Best Friends of the Gallery Volunteers

PUBLICATIONS & CONTENT DEVELOPMENT
Lam Yong Ling
Ong Zhen Min
Wong Jia Min

CURATORIAL PROGRAMMES
Erica Lai
Rose Wei

EDUCATION
Elaine Chan
Shaherah Bin Arshad

LEGAL COUNSEL
Huang Meili

MARKETING & COMMUNICATIONS
Yvonne Lim
Amelia Loh
Cheryl Teo
Tuan Szi Yi
Kerrie Wee

PARTNERSHIP DEVELOPMENT
Koh Li Xin
Nicole Alison Lim
Puan Mei Yi

PROGRAMMES
Tamares Goh
Lim Shengen
Selena Tan

SPECIAL THANKS
Sam Rauch of Tanya Bonakdar Gallery